THE END OF
MODERN HISTORY
IN THE
MIDDLE EAST

HERBERT AND JANE DWIGHT WORKING GROUP
ON ISLAMISM AND THE INTERNATIONAL ORDER

Many of the writings associated with this
Working Group will be published by the Hoover Institution.
Materials published to date, or in production, are listed below.

ESSAYS

Saudi Arabia and the New Strategic Landscape
Joshua Teitelbaum

Islamism and the Future of the Christians of the Middle East
Habib C. Malik

Syria through Jihadist Eyes: A Perfect Enemy
Nibras Kazimi

The Ideological Struggle for Pakistan
Ziad Haider

BOOKS

Freedom or Terror: Europe Faces Jihad
Russell A. Berman

The Myth of the Great Satan: A New Look at America's Relations with Iran
Abbas Milani

Torn Country: Turkey between Secularism and Islamism
Zeyno Baran

Islamic Extremism and the War of Ideas: Lessons from Indonesia
John Hughes

Crosswinds: The Way of Saudi Arabia
Fouad Ajami

The End of Modern History in the Middle East
Bernard Lewis

The Wave: Man, God, and the Ballot Box in the Middle East
Reuel Marc Gerecht

Trial of a Thousand Years: World Order and Islamism
Charles Hill

Jihad in the Arabian Sea
Camille Pecastaing

HERBERT AND JANE DWIGHT WORKING GROUP ON ISLAMISM AND THE INTERNATIONAL ORDER

THE END OF MODERN HISTORY IN THE MIDDLE EAST

Bernard Lewis

HOOVER INSTITUTION PRESS

STANFORD UNIVERSITY | STANFORD, CALIFORNIA

www.hoover.org

Hoover Institution Press Publication No. 604

Hoover Institution at Leland Stanford Junior University, Stanford, California 94305-6010

First printing 2011
17 16 15 14 13 12 11   9 8 7 6 5 4 3 2 1

Manufactured in the United States of America

The paper used in this publication meets the minimum Requirements of the American National Standard for Information Sciences—Permanence of Paper for Printed Library Materials, ANSI/NISO Z39.48-1992. ♾

Cataloging-in-Publication Data is available from the Library of Congress.
ISBN 978-0-8179-1294-9 (cloth : alk. paper)
ISBN 978-0-8179-1296-3 (e-book)

The Hoover Institution gratefully acknowledges the following individuals and foundations for their significant support of the

HERBERT AND JANE DWIGHT WORKING GROUP ON ISLAMISM AND THE INTERNATIONAL ORDER:

Herbert and Jane Dwight
Stephen Bechtel Foundation
Lynde and Harry Bradley Foundation
Mr. and Mrs. Clayton W. Frye Jr.
Lakeside Foundation

CONTENTS

F OR DECADES, THE THEMES of the Hoover Institution have revolved around the broad concerns of
political and economic and individual freedom. The
Cold War that engaged and challenged our nation during
the twentieth century guided a good deal of Hoover's work,
including its archival accumulation and research studies.
The steady output of work on the communist world offers
durable testimonies to that time, and struggle. But there
is no repose from history's exertions, and no sooner had
communism left the stage of history than a huge challenge
arose in the broad lands of the Islamic world. A brief
respite, and a meandering road, led from the fall of the Berlin Wall on 11/9 in 1989 to 9/11. Hoover's newly launched
project, the Herbert and Jane Dwight Working Group on
Islamism and the International Order, is our contribution
to a deeper understanding of the struggle in the Islamic
world between order and its nemesis, between Muslims
keen to protect the rule of reason and the gains of modernity, and those determined to deny the Islamic world its
place in the modern international order of states. The
United States is deeply engaged, and dangerously exposed,
in the Islamic world, and we see our working group as part
and parcel of the ongoing confrontation with the radical

Islamists who have declared war on the states in their midst, on American power and interests, and on the very order of the international state system.

The Islamists are doubtless a minority in the world of Islam. But they are a determined breed. Their world is the Islamic emirate, led by self-styled "emirs and mujahedeen in the path of God" and legitimized by the pursuit of the caliphate that collapsed with the end of the Ottoman Empire in 1924. These masters of terror and their foot soldiers have made it increasingly difficult to integrate the world of Islam into modernity. In the best of worlds, the entry of Muslims into modern culture and economics would have presented difficulties of no small consequence: the strictures on women, the legacy of humiliation and self-pity, the outdated educational systems, and an explosive demography that is forever at war with social and economic gains. But the borders these warriors of the faith have erected between Islam and "the other" are particularly forbidding. The lands of Islam were the lands of a crossroads civilization, trading routes and mixed populations. The Islamists have waged war, and a brutally effective one it has to be conceded, against that civilizational inheritance. The leap into the modern world economy as attained by China and India in recent years will be virtually impossible in a culture that feeds off belligerent self-pity, and endlessly calls for wars of faith.

The war of ideas with radical Islamism is inescapably central to this Hoover endeavor. The strategic context of this clash, the landscape of that Greater Middle East, is the other pillar. We face three layers of danger in the heartland of the Islamic world: states that have succumbed to the sway of terrorists in which state authority no longer exists (Afghanistan, Somalia, and Yemen), dictatorial regimes that suppress their people at home and pursue deadly weapons of mass destruction and adventurism abroad (Iraq under Saddam Hussein, the Iranian theocracy), and "enabler" regimes, such as the ones in Egypt and Saudi Arabia, which export their own problems with radical Islamism to other parts of the Islamic world and beyond. In this context, the task of reversing Islamist radicalism and of reforming and strengthening the state across the entire Muslim world—the Middle East, Africa, as well as South, Southeast, and Central Asia—is the greatest strategic challenge of the twenty-first century. The essential starting point is detailed knowledge of our enemy.

Thus, the working group will draw on the intellectual resources of Hoover and Stanford and on an array of scholars and practitioners from elsewhere in the United States, from the Middle East, and the broader world of Islam. The scholarship on contemporary Islam can now be read with discernment. A good deal of it, produced in the immediate aftermath of 9/11, was not particularly deep and did not stand the test of time and events. We, however, are in the favorable position of a "second generation" assessment of that Islamic material. Our scholars and experts can report, in a detailed, authoritative way, on Islam within the Arabian Peninsula, on trends within Egyptian Islam, on the struggle between the Kemalist secular tradition in Turkey and the new Islamists, particularly the fight for the loyalty of European Islam between those who accept the canon, and the discipline, of modernism and those who do not.

Arabs and Muslims need not be believers in American exceptionalism, but our hope is to engage them in this contest of ideas. We will not necessarily aim at producing primary scholarship, but such scholarship may materialize in that our participants are researchers who know their subjects intimately. We see our critical output as essays accessible to a broader audience, primers about matters that require explication, op-eds, writings that will become part of the public debate, and short, engaging books that can illuminate the choices and the struggles in modern Islam.

We see this endeavor as a faithful reflection of the values that animate a decent, moderate society. We know the travails of modern Islam, and this working group will be unsparing in depicting them. But we also know that the battle for modern Islam is not yet lost, that there are brave men and women fighting to retrieve their faith from the extremists. Some of our participants will themselves be intellectuals and public figures who have stood up to the pressure. The working group will be unapologetic about America's role in the Muslim world. A power that laid to waste religious tyranny in Afghanistan and despotism in Iraq, that came to the rescue of the Muslims in the Balkans when they appeared all but doomed, has given much to those burdened populations. We haven't always understood Islam and Muslims—hence this inquiry. But it is a given of the working group that the pursuit of modernity and human welfare, and of the rule of law and reason, in Islamic lands is the common ground between America and contemporary Islam.

FOUAD AJAMI

Senior Fellow, Hoover Institution
Cochairman, Herbert and Jane Dwight Working Group
on Islamism and the International Order

ACKNOWLEDGMENTS

I WOULD LIKE TO NOTE that an earlier, shorter version my first chapter, "The End of Modern History in the Middle East," was printed in London in 1997 for limited private circulation under the title "Predictions."

My second chapter, "Propaganda in the Middle East," also appeared in earlier forms: as a short paper entitled "Propaganda in the Pre-Modern Middle East: A Preliminary Classification," it was published by the Hebrew University of Jerusalem, Faculty of Humanities, in their series Jerusalem Studies in Arabic and Islam, Volume 25 (2001), pp. 1–14. It was later reprinted in my book *From Babel to Dragomans: Interpreting the Middle East*, Oxford University Press, New York, 2004, pp. 97–113.

"Iran: Haman or Cyrus?" is based on the transcription of a lecture. It has been available on some websites but has not been published in printed form.

Chapter Four, "The New Anti-Semitism," is based on an article published in the *American Scholar*, Vol. 75, No. 1, Winter 2006, pp. 25–36.

I would like to thank those publishers and individuals associated with the earlier iterations of the chapters included in this present volume for their cooperation.

Apart from that, I would like to express my profound thanks and appreciation to Fouad Ajami, for proposing, encouraging, and accomplishing the publication of this book.

The *Historian's* Vision:
The *Craft* of Bernard Lewis

by FOUAD AJAMI

F ATE—OR, MORE APPROPRIATELY, HISTORY— decreed his American journey and the direction it would take. Historian Bernard Lewis had come to Princeton from London, at the age of 58, in 1974, to do the work of Orientalism, which had gained him scholarly renown. But there would be no academic seclusion for him in the years after. The lands of Islam whose languages and cultures he knew with such intimacy would soon be set ablaze. And his adopted country, the bearer of the imperial mantle shed by his own Britannia, would in time make an honored place for him, and all but anoint him its guide into those burning grounds of the Islamic world. He would become the oracle of this new age of the Americans in the lands of the Arab and Islamic worlds.

In the normal course of things, America is not a country given to excessive deference to historians and to the claims of history, for the past is truly a foreign country here. But

the past three decades were no normal time, and Mr. Lewis
no typical historian. He knew and worked the archives, it
is true; and he mastered the languages of "the East,"
standing at the peak of his academic guild. But there is
more to him than that: He is, through and through, a man
of public affairs. He saw the coming of a war, a great civilizational struggle, and was to show no timidity about the
facts of this war. "I'll teach you differences," Kent says to
one of Lear's servants. And Mr. Lewis has been teaching
us differences. He knew Islam's splendor and its periods
of enlightenment; he had celebrated the "dignity and
meaning" it gave to "drab impoverished lives." He would
not hesitate, then, to look into—and to name—the darkness and the rage that have overcome so many of its adherents in recent times.

WE ANOINT SAGES when we need them; at times we let them
say, on our behalf, the sorts of things we know and intuit
but don't say, the sorts of things we glimpse through the
darkness but don't fully see. It was thus in the time of the
great illusion, in the lost decade of the 1990s, when history
had presumably "ended," that Bernard Lewis came forth to
tell us, in a seminal essay, "The Roots of Muslim Rage" (in
The Atlantic, September 1990), that our luck had run out,
that an old struggle between "Christendom" and Islam was
gathering force. (Note the name given the Western world;
it is vintage Lewis, this naming of worlds and drawing of
borders—and differences.) It was the time of commerce

and globalism; the "modernists" had the run of the decade, and a historian's dark premonitions about a thwarted civilization wishing to avenge the slights and wounds of centuries would not carry the day. Mr. Lewis was the voice of conservatives, a brooding pessimist, in the time of a sublime faith in things new and untried. It was he, in that 1990 article, who gave us the notion of a "clash of civilizations" that Samuel Huntington would popularize, with due attribution to Bernard Lewis.

The rage of Islam was no mystery to Mr. Lewis. To no great surprise, it issued out of his respect for the Muslim logic of things. For 14 centuries, he wrote, Islam and Christendom had feuded and fought across a bloody and shifting frontier, their enmity a "series of attacks and counter-attacks, jihads and crusades, conquests and reconquests." For nearly a millennium, Islam had the upper hand. The new faith conquered Syria, Palestine, Egypt and North Africa—old Christian lands, it should be recalled. It struck into Europe, established dominions in Sicily, Spain, Portugal and in parts of France. Before the tide turned, there had been panic in Europe that Christendom was doomed. In a series of letters written from Constantinople between 1555 and 1560, Ogier Ghiselin de Busbecq, imperial ambassador to the court of Suleyman the Magnificent, anguished over Europe's fate; he was sure that the Turks were about to "fly at our throats, supported by the might of the whole East." Europe, he worried, was squandering its wealth, "seeking the Indies and the Antipodes across vast fields of ocean, in search of gold."

But Busbecq, we know, had it wrong. The threat of Islam was turned back. The wealth brought back from the New World helped turn the terms of trade against Islam. Europe's confidence soared. The great turning point came in 1683, when a Turkish siege of Vienna ended in failure and defeat. With the Turks on the run, the terms of engagement between Europe and Islam were transformed. Russia overthrew the Tatar yoke; there was the *Reconquista* in the Iberian Peninsula. Instead of winning every war, Mr. Lewis observes, the Muslims were *losing* every war. Britain, France, the Netherlands and Russia all soon spilled into Islamic lands. "Europe and her daughters" now disposed of the fate of Muslim domains. Americans and Europeans may regard this new arrangement of power as natural. But Mr. Lewis has been relentless in his admonition that Muslims were under no obligation to accept the new order of things.

A pain afflicts modern Islam—the loss of power. And Mr. Lewis has a keen sense of the Muslim redeemers and would-be avengers who promise to alter Islam's place in the world. This pain, the historian tells us, derives from Islam's early success, from the very triumph of the prophet Muhammad. Moses had not been allowed to enter the promised land; he had led his people through wilderness. Jesus had been crucified. But Muhammad prevailed and governed. The faith he bequeathed his followers would forever insist on the oneness of religion and politics. Where Christians are enjoined in their scripture to "render unto Caesar the things which are Caesar's and unto God the things which are God's," no such demarcation is drawn in the theory and practice of Islam.

It was vintage Lewis—reading the sources, in this case a marginal Arabic newspaper published out of London, *Al-Quds Al-Arabi*, in February of 1998—to come across a declaration of war on the United States by a self-designated holy warrior he had "never heard of," Osama bin Laden. In one of those essays that reveal the historian's eye for things that matter, "A License to Kill," published in the November/December 1998 issue of *Foreign Affairs*, Mr. Lewis renders into sublime English prose the declaration of bin Laden and gives it its exegesis. The historian might have never heard of bin Laden, but the terrorist from Arabia practically walks out of the pages of Mr. Lewis's own histories. Consider this passage from the Arabian plotter: "Since God laid down the Arabian Peninsula, created its desert, and surrounded it with seas, no calamity has ever befallen it like these crusader hosts that have spread in it like locusts, eating its fruits and destroying its verdure; and this at a time when the nations contend against Muslims like diners jostling around a bowl of food. . . . By God's leave, we call on every Muslim who believes in God and hopes for reward to obey God's command to kill the Americans and plunder their possessions whenever he finds them and whenever he can."

Three years later, the furies of bin Laden, and the cadence and content of his language—straight out of the annals of older wars of faith—would remake our world. There would come Mr. Lewis's way now waves of people willing to believe. They would read into his works the bewildering ways and furies of preachers and plotters and foot soldiers hurling themselves against the order of the West. Timing was cruel—and exquisite. The historian's book *What Went Wrong?* was already in galleys by 9/11. He had not written it for the storm. He had all but anticipated what was to come. This diagnosis of Islam's malady would become a best seller. In a different setting, Mr. Lewis had written of history's power, "Make no mistake, those who are unwilling to confront the past will be unable to understand the present and unfit to face the future." We were witnessing an epic jumbling of past and present. It was no fault of this historian that we had placed our bet on the death of the past.

Mr. Lewis has lived a long and engaged life, caught up in the great issues of war and diplomacy—and may he be with us as far as the eye can see, as long as life and good health permit. Some of his detractors, with an excessive belief in his talismans, have attributed to the historian all sorts of large historical deeds. For some, he is the godfather of the accommodation of years past between Turkey and Israel. For others, he inspired the Iraq war, transmitting to Vice President Dick Cheney his faith in the Iraq campaign as the spearhead of an effort to reform the Arab world. In more recent writings on the historian, George W. Bush's "diplomacy of freedom" in Arab-Muslim lands is laid at Mr. Lewis's doorstep. The president was seen, in one account, with a marked-up copy of a Lewis article. We had come to a great irony: the conservative Orientalist holding out democratic hope for Iraq and its Arab neighbors, while his liberal critics were asserting the built-in authoritarianism of the Arab political tradition. In truth, he was against a military invasion of Iraq. He was in favor of the establishment of an independent government of a free Iraq in the northern zone.

For Bernard Lewis, there is something now of the closing of a circle. As a young man, he began military service in the tank regiment and was transferred from there to military intelligence during the Second World War, working for British intelligence between 1940 and 1945. The young medievalist was pressed into modern government work, and that experience gave him his taste for contemporary political affairs. This new war is something of a return to his beginnings. For an immensely gregarious man of unfailing wit and personal optimism, a darkness runs through his view of the future of the Western democracies. "In 1940, we knew who we were, we knew who the enemy was, we knew the dangers and the issues," he told me when I pressed him for a reading of the struggle against Islamic radicalism. "In our island, we knew we would prevail, that the Americans would be drawn into the fight. It is different today. We don't know who we are, we don't know the issues, and we still do not understand the nature of the enemy."

The Muslim Brotherhood in Egypt, which once translated one of Mr. Lewis's books into Arabic, said that his book was "the work of a candid friend or an honest enemy." Either way, the Brotherhood said, it was the work of "someone who disdains falsification." And this, to me and to his countless readers, runs to the core of this historian's craft—the aversion to falsification. He has been, always, a man of his own civilization and convictions—a fact that accounts for the deep reservoirs of reverence felt for him in many Arab and other Muslim lands. In the American academy, he may be swimming against the currents of postmodernism and postcolonial history; he has given up his membership in the Middle East Studies Association, of which he was a founding member. But countless Arab and Iranian and Turkish readers recognize their tormented civilization in what he has written. They know that he has not come to the material of their history driven by bad faith, or by a desire for dominion. They take him at his word, a man of the Anglo-Saxon world, convinced that the ways of the West today carry with them the hopes of other civilizations. In one of his many splendid books, *Cultures in Conflict: Christians, Muslims, and Jews in the Age of Discovery* (1995), he gave voice to both his fears and to his faith: "It may be that Western culture will indeed go: the lack of conviction of many of those who should be its defenders and the passionate intensity of its accusers may well join to complete its destruction. But if it does go, the men and women of all the continents will thereby be impoverished and endangered."

EDWARD GIBBON once called the historian's "I" the "most disgusting of pronouns." In the main we see very little of that pronoun in Mr. Lewis's work. But in the academy he belongs to the ages. He is the peer, and inheritor, of the great Western scholars of Islam—the Hungarian Ignaz Goldziher (1850–1921), the Dutch Christiaan Snouck Hurgronje (1857–1936), the French Louis Massignon (1883–1962), the British Thomas Arnold (1864–1930) and Mr. Lewis's own teacher, Sir Hamilton Gibb (1895–1971). Mr. Lewis took to the East to understand his own world because, as he tells us, Western civilization "did not spring like Aphrodite from the sea foam." He wanted to get to the mainsprings of Western civilization.

I shall set aside the ban on that "most disgusting of pronouns." I came to know Bernard Lewis the year he made his passage to America, on the Princeton campus. I was then at the beginning of my academic career, obscure and justifiably anxious. Mr. Lewis was one of the academic gods. I approached him with awe. But his grace was our bridge. I was of the old world he studied; he was keen to know the name of my ancestral village in southern Lebanon. I told him it was an obscure place without history, and gave him its name. He offered me an invitation to examine his archives and said that he had the land deeds of that remote hamlet. It has been like this with Bernard Lewis: we travel by the light of his work. He weaves for us a web between past and present, and he can pick out, over distant horizons, storms sure to reach us before long.

A book of memoirs is promised; we shall be given the chance to see Bernard Lewis shedding his reticence about the personal pronoun. In this endeavor, we offer four narratives of this singular figure in the Western academy. In

our time, the work on political Islam began with Bernard
Lewis and his researches; he is doubtless the intellectual
godfather of this intellectual enterprise. It was in a high secular world, proud of its modernism, indifferent to matters
of religious faith, that Bernard Lewis penned one of those
memorable essays, "The Return of Islam," in 1976. He lived
to see more of history's compliance than he could have ever
hoped for, or wanted. This field of study, now ours, is his
by right of toil and labor.

The End *of*
Modern History
in the
Middle East

CHAPTER ONE

The End of
Modern History
in the Middle East

ACCORDING TO A CONVENTION commonly agreed upon among historians, the modern history of the Middle East begins at the turn of the nineteenth century, when a French expeditionary force commanded by General Napoleon Bonaparte invaded and conquered Egypt and stayed there until it was forced to leave by a squadron of the Royal Navy commanded by Admiral Horatio Nelson. This was not the first Western advance against the previously dominant power of Islam. But it was the first incursion from the West into the heartlands of the Islamic world.

Bonaparte's arrival and still more his departure demonstrated two important facts: that even a small Western force could conquer, occupy and rule one of these heartlands without serious difficulty and that only another Western force could get them out.

This began a period during which ultimate power over, and with it responsibility for, what happened in this region resided elsewhere; when the basic theme of international relations and of much else in the Middle East was shaped by the rivalries of non–Middle Eastern states. These rivalries went through several successive phases—interference, intervention, penetration, domination and, in the final phase, sometimes reluctant, sometimes relieved departure. From time to time the actors in the drama changed and the script was modified, but until the final phase the basic pattern remained the same. In that final act of this drama, the two external superpowers whose rivalry dominated the Middle East were the Soviet Union and the United States. In their purposes and their methods, they were very different, both from their predecessors and from each other.

Future historians of the region may well agree on a new convention of periodization—that the era in Middle Eastern history that was opened by Napoleon and Nelson was closed by George H. W. Bush and Mikhail Gorbachev. In the crisis of 1990–91 precipitated by Saddam Hussein's invasion of Kuwait, neither of the two superpowers played the imperial role which tradition and popular expectation assigned to it; the one because it could not, the other because it would not.

Moscow, once so great a force in Middle Eastern affairs, could neither restrain nor rescue Saddam Hussein. Washington, having freed Kuwait from occupation and Saudi Arabia from the threat of invasion, had accomplished its war aims and unilaterally declared a cease-fire, leaving Saddam's regime intact and permitting him, with only minor impediments, to crush his domestic opponents and in due course resume his policies.

As long as the Soviet Union existed, and as long as the Cold War was the main theme of foreign policy, American presence in the Middle East was part of a global strategy designed to cope with a global confrontation. With the ending of that confrontation, such a strategy became unnecessary. No discernible strategy has yet emerged to replace it. The breakup of the Soviet Union brought another important consequence—the emergence of eight new sovereign independent states in Transcaucasia and Central Asia. Two of these, Georgia and Armenia, are Christian; the rest, Azerbaijan, Kazakstan, Kyrgyzstan, Turkmenistan, Uzbekistan and Tajikistan are predominantly Muslim. All these countries are part of the historic Middle East, linked to it by a thousand ties of culture, language and history. The Tajik language is a form of Persian; the other five Muslim states use languages related to Turkish. The Turks, Persians and Afghans show increasing interest in their newly liberated kinsfolk across the former Soviet frontier. They are also interested in those other Muslim peoples—Tatars, Bashkirs, Chechens, Circassians and others, who remain within the Russian federation. The same interest is beginning to extend to the Muslims of Chinese Central Asia, notably the Uyghurs, a Muslim people speaking a Turkic language.

The emergence of a world of Turkic states, like the Arab world that emerged from the breakup of the British and French empires, will be increasingly important in the decades to come and will have a significant effect on the Middle East to which they are now returning. But there are differences between the two cases. With a few exceptions, notably, Algeria and Aden, British and French rule in the Arab world was indirect and of brief duration. The Transcaucasian and Central Asian territories were annexed by the czars and retained by the Soviets under a thin veneer of federalism. Their experience of imperial rule was in many ways profoundly different from that of the Arabs. Their efforts to disentangle themselves from the embrace of their former masters offer some similarities to the early stages of Arab independence. But they are dealing with Moscow, not with London or Paris; with a land-based power, not a maritime and commercial ascendancy. The course and perhaps the outcome of their struggle for true independence will surely reflect these differences.

In that historical interlude between the fall of the Berlin Wall and the terror attacks in the United States on September 11, 2001, Russia was out of the game and likely to remain so for some years to come; America was reluctant to return. This meant that in many significant respects the situation reverted to what it was before. Outside powers had interests in the region, both strategic and economic; they could from time to time interfere in Middle Eastern affairs or even influence their course. But their role was no longer to be one of domination or decision.

Many in the Middle East had difficulty in adjusting themselves to the new situation created by the departure of the imperial powers. For the first time in almost 200 years, the rulers and to some extent the peoples of the Middle East are having to accept final responsibility for their own affairs;

to recognize their own mistakes and to accept the consequences. This was difficult to internalize, even to perceive, after so long a period. For the entire lifetimes of those who formulate and conduct policy at the present time and of their predecessors for many generations, the vital decisions were made elsewhere, ultimate control lay elsewhere, and the principal task of statesmanship and diplomacy was as far as possible to avoid or reduce the dangers of this situation and to exploit such opportunities as it might from time to time offer. It is very difficult to forsake the habits not just of a lifetime but of a whole era of history. The difficulty is much greater when alien cultural, social and economic preeminence continues and even increases, despite the ending of alien political and military domination.

Military and to a growing extent political intervention by the West had seemingly come to an end, but the impact of its science and culture, its technology, amenities and institutions was, if anything, on the rise—here as in other parts of the non-Western world.

In these circumstances, it is natural that Middle Easterners should continue to assume—and proceed on the assumption—that real responsibility and decisions still lie elsewhere. In its crudest form, this belief leads to wild and strange conspiracy theories directed against those whom they regard as their enemies—Israel, and more generally the Jews, the United States, and more generally the West. No theory is too absurd to be asserted or too preposterous to be widely and instantly believed. Even among more responsible statesmen and analysts, a similar belief in alien power, albeit in a less crude form, often seems to guide both analysis and policy. Some even go so far as to invite outside intervention, presumably in the belief that only outside powers have the capacity to make and enforce decisions. A case in point is the constant appeal to the United States to involve itself in the Arab-Israel conflict, oddly coupled with the repeated accusation of "American imperialism." This particular charge reveals a misunderstanding of either America or imperialism or, more probably, both. The term imperialism might not unjustly be applied to some of the processes by which the original 13 states were increased to the present-day 50, but as a description of American policy in the Middle East at the present day, it is absurdly wrong. When the Romans went to Britain 2,000 years ago, or when the British went to India 300 years ago, an "exit strategy" did not figure prominently among their concerns.

This strategic landscape was altered by the terror attack on American soil on September 11, 2001. In the aftermath of that terrible day, American forces were dispatched to Afghanistan, and before long, to Iraq. The American policy of benign neglect of this region was brought to a swift end. American home security was at stake. A war on terror had begun, and the United States was pulled into hitherto unimaginable obligations and dangers. There had previously been no great debate about this new burden in Muslim lands. The shock of the attacks of 9/11 convinced American policy makers that a more ambitious policy was in order. In time, the thought would emerge that it was urgent to push for a wholesale reform in Arab and Islamic

lands. Reform was not easy, but the risks of the status quo—
repressive political orders, cultures of unreason and scape-
goating—inspired this push into the Islamic world with a
new sense of both urgency and legitimacy.

This was not what those who had perpetrated the terror
attacks had in mind. Their leader, the Saudi financier and
jihadist Osama bin Laden, was sure of the weakness of
American resolve. Three years before he dispatched the
death pilots of 9/11, in an interview with John Miller of
ABC News on May 28, 1998, he gave voice to this senti-
ment. "We have seen in the last decade the decline of the
American government and the weakness of the American
soldier, who is ready to wage cold wars and unprepared to
fight long wars," he said. "This was proven in Beirut when
the Marines fled after two explosions. It also proves they
can run in less than 24 hours and this was also repeated in
Somalia. . . . [Our] youth were surprised at the low morale
of the American soldiers. . . . After a few blows, they ran in
defeat. . . . They forgot about being the world leader and
the leader of the new world order. They left, dragging their
corpses in their shameful defeat."

As he saw it, the Islamic fighters in Afghanistan had
defeated and destroyed the mighty Soviet Union. Dealing
with the Untied States would be a much easier task. This
was his belief and the source of his resolve. The same message appears in several other statements—that Americans
had become soft and pampered, unable or unwilling to
stand up and fight. It was a lesson bin Laden extracted from
American responses to previous attacks: he expected more

of the same. There would be fierce words and perhaps the United States would launch a missile or two to some remote places, but there would be little else in terms of retaliation.

It was a natural error. Nothing in his background or his experience would enable him to understand that a major policy change could result from an election. As we now know, it was also a deadly error. What in fact followed—the campaign in Afghanistan, the declaration of war against the "axis of evil," and the war against the Iraqi regime of Saddam Hussein—must have come as a shock to him and to his various sponsors and helpers. The assault of 9/11 was surely intended as the opening salvo of a war of terror that would continue until its objectives were obtained—that is, the eviction of the United States from the world of Islam and, most important, the overthrow of the Arab regimes seen by the West as friendly and by al-Qaeda and many of their own subjects as renegades from Islam and puppets of America.

The logic of the jihadists had backfired. Rather than head for the exits, America was to dig in for a deeper presence in Arab and Islamic lands. If this was imperialism, it was imperialism of a defensive kind.

Those who accuse the West and more particularly the United States of "imperialist designs" on the Middle East are tilting against shadows from the past. There is however another charge with more substance—that of cultural penetration.

American culture differs from all its predecessors in two important respects. First, it is independent of political control and extends far beyond the areas of American political dominance or even influence, as for example in Islamic

Iran or Communist China. Second, it is in a profound sense popular. Previous cultural expansions were limited to political and intellectual elites. American popular culture appeals to every element of the population and especially to the young. It also brings a special message to elements disempowered in the traditional order, notably women. Not surprisingly, therefore, it is perceived as a mortal threat both by the defenders of tradition and by the exponents of fundamentalist ideologies. How that threat is perceived is clear from the Ayatollah Khomeini's repeated characterization of the United States as "the Great Satan." No intelligence service is needed to interpret this epithet—just a copy of the Qur'ān. The last verses, the best known along with the first, talk about Satan, describing him as "the insidious tempter who whispers in the hearts of men." Satan is neither a conqueror nor an exploiter. He is a seducer, most dangerous when he smiles.

The challenge of Western culture has been a major theme in Middle Eastern debate for almost two centuries. American popular culture presents this challenge in its most recent and also its most pervasive form. Middle Eastern rulers, leaders and thinkers have offered and will no doubt continue to offer various responses to this challenge—imitate, adopt, adapt, absorb, or complain, denounce, reject.

FAITH AND FREEDOM

When General Bonaparte arrived in 1798, there were only two sovereign states in the Middle East: Turkey and Iran.

Today, these are resuming their historic roles as the major powers of the region. The present regimes in both, were founded by revolution—the secular republic of Turkey and the Islamic republic of Iran. Both were inspired by revolutionary ideologies which might be named after their founders as Kemalism and Khomeinism. And both ideologies, albeit in very different ways, are under attack at home.

Today, increasing numbers of Middle Easterners, disillusioned with past ideals and—in many countries—alienated from their present rulers, are turning their thoughts or their loyalties to one or other of these two ideologies—liberal democracy and Islamic fundamentalism. Each offers a reasoned diagnosis of the ills of the region and a prescription for its cure.

In this struggle, fundamentalism disposes of several advantages. It uses language that is familiar and intelligible, appealing to the vast mass of the population in a Muslim country. At a time of economic deprivation, social dislocation and political oppression, many are ready to believe that these evils are a result of alien and infidel machinations and that the remedy is a return to the original, authentic way of Islam. The fundamentalists also have an immense advantage over other opposition groups in that the mosques and their personnel provide them with a network for meeting and communication which even the most tyrannical of governments cannot suppress or entirely control. Indeed, tyrannical regimes help their fundamentalist opponents by eliminating competing oppositions.

The exponents of democracy, in contrast, offer a program and a language that are unfamiliar and, for many, unintelligible. They have the further disadvantage that the name of democracy and those of the parties and parliaments through which it operates have been tarnished in the eyes of many Muslims by the corrupt and inept regimes that used these names in the recent past. In contrast, appeals in the name of God and the Prophet to cleanse society by restoring his holy law have a force and immediacy unattainable by democrats whose arguments, examples, and even vocabulary are recognizably alien. An Arabic loanword like *dimuqratiyya* lacks the resonance of *shari'a*.

But things are changing. In countries where fundamentalists are a powerful force and still more in those where they rule, Muslims are learning to distinguish between Islam as an ethical religion and way of life and fundamentalism as a ruthless political ideology. In countries where they oppose the regime, such as Egypt and Algeria, fundamentalist terrorists have shown a callous brutality that shocks and repels ordinary, decent believers. In countries where they rule, such as Iran and at times Sudan, they are, perhaps inevitably, disappointing the high hopes that they evoked. The regime of the mullahs in Iran is not noticeably less corrupt than that which it replaced. It is more efficiently and pervasively repressive, and increasing numbers of Iranians, in desperation, are turning against Islamic fundamentalism and sometimes even against Islam itself. Many good Muslims in Iran and elsewhere see in this a mortal danger to their faith and civilization, and there is a growing movement which challenges Islamic fundamentalism, not in the name of secularism, but in the name of Islam. The most serious challenge to the Iranian regime may well come from within its own ranks.

The fundamentalist regimes are also failing by the more palpable test of performance. In Iran, the effects of fundamentalist rule will for a while be palliated by the availability of money from oil and the remarkably skillful use made of this resource in dealing with foreign governments and business corporations. But it is only a palliative, and of limited duration. Elsewhere, where no such palliative exists, the most visible effects of fundamentalist rule are poverty, tyranny and unending internal warfare. The programs and activities of fundamentalist oppositions in other countries promise nothing better. It is becoming increasingly clear that whatever political and propaganda successes they may achieve, fundamentalist movements—and governments—have no real understanding and therefore no solutions for the pressing problems of modern society. Their diagnosis is moral—society has been corrupted and enfeebled by pagan and infidel ways, especially in sexual matters; their remedy is legal—the restoration and strict enforcement of the holy law, that is to say, of those parts and those interpretations that form the basis of fundamentalist ideology. The importance of morality and of law is immense and obvious, but it does not suffice in confronting the pressing economic and social problems of the modern world. The resulting tensions grow daily more serious. They will become critical if these problems persist until the time when oil revenues are no longer available.

A triumph of Islamic fundamentalism would have far-reaching consequences outside as well as inside the region and would evoke sharp responses from other religions—

and other fundamentalisms. From the advent of Islam in the seventh century, Muslim jihad wrested vast lands from Christendom and incorporated them in the realm of Islam. After several centuries, Christianity—a religion with a pacifist core—at last reacted with a jihad of its own, variously known as the Reconquest and the Crusades.

It could happen again. Most Christians—even in the highest ecclesiastical hierarchies—have abandoned the triumphalism and militancy of their forebears. But Muslim triumphalism and militancy could bring a revival, and there are signs that this has already begun. The problem begins with the position of non-Muslims in Muslim states. The very real tolerance once accorded by Muslim states to non-Muslims living under their rule was predicated on their acceptance of the supremacy of Islam and the primacy of the Muslims. When modern ideas disrupt the old consensus, the old tolerance comes under severe strain and is often broken. Attacks on Christians in Iran, in Egypt, in Algeria, in Sudan and elsewhere are reviving old and deep-rooted fears. They have also prompted, in some quarters, a perception of Islam as the new world menace, taking the place vacated by the defunct Soviet Union and its dead communist creed. For the time being at least, this view is an exaggeration of the strength of Muslim militancy and a misinterpretation of the nature of Islam. But the warnings of a new religious response to militant Islam are already there.

In the struggle between democracy and fundamentalism for power in Muslim lands, the democrats suffer from a very serious disadvantage. As democrats, they are obliged to allow the fundamentalists equal opportunity to conduct propaganda and to contend for power. If they fail in this duty, they are violating the very essence of their own democratic creed. Paradoxically, it is the Western concern for democratic freedom, even at the cost of Western values and of freedom itself, that sometimes prevents the Muslim secularists from dealing with this problem in the traditional way.

The fundamentalists are under no such disability. For them, winning an election is one of several possible roads to power—and it is a one-way road on which there is no turning back. Fundamentalists, speaking at home, do not even pretend any commitment to democratic choice and make it clear that, once in power, they would in no circumstances be willing to depart by the road through which they came. On the contrary, it would be their solemn duty to eradicate elements and ideas contrary to the law of God and to enforce that law against all transgressors. The strength of the democrats, and the corresponding weakness of the fundamentalists, is that the former have a program of development and betterment, while the latter offer only a return to a mythologized past. The problem is that the weaknesses of the democrats are immediate and obvious; their strengths are long-term and, for many, obscure.

Some speak of a possible compromise between the rival extremes—a type of representative democracy not formally secular, in which a moderate but not fundamentalist Islam might play the role of the established churches in Britain and Scandinavia or of the Christian democratic parties in continental European countries. There is little sign of any such compromise as yet, and at the present time it seems unlikely that any will emerge. But the idea of a combination of freedom and faith in which neither one excludes the other has achieved some results among Christians and Jews and may yet provide a workable solution for the problems of political Islam.

Until recently, one would have said that the best prospects for the emergence of such a compromise are in Turkey, a country in which most of the population are committed Muslims and in which a parliamentary democracy—albeit with difficulties and reversals—has now functioned for more than half a century. Turkey was the first Muslim country to establish and maintain such a democracy; it was also the first in which the leader of an avowedly Islamic party, Necmettin Erbakan, became prime minister by electoral and constitutional means. He was pushed out of power by the military; his party, Refah (Welfare), was banned. But younger Islamists found their way to power, again through the ballot box. A former mayor of Istanbul, Recep Tayyip Erdogan, picked up where Erbakan had faltered. Now it is becoming clear that the party he leads, the Justice and Development Party, is not just Islamic; it is, for many of its adherents, fundamentalist. The party press reveals attitudes that are anti-Christian, anti-Semitic, anti-Western and, more generally, antiliberal and antimodern. Its leaders and spokesmen show affinities—and form alliances—with the most extreme elements in Iran and in some of the Arab countries.

The alarm caused by these developments is increased by reports of the spread of fundamentalist activities in the political, economic and cultural spheres, and, still more dangerous, by the fundamentalists' acquisition of large quantities of guns and other weapons. As secular elements in the state and more particularly in the armed forces speak darkly of a showdown, the fear is widely expressed that Turkey might become another Algeria or, more plausibly, another Iran. If that happens, the trouble would certainly spread rapidly, both northwards to the ex-Soviet Turkic states and southwards to the ex-Ottoman Arab states.

But this is not inevitable. The Turks, unlike all their Muslim neighbors except Iran, have long experience of sovereign independence. They also have a unique experience of democratic change. One may hope that the Turkish political class will recover the skill and steadiness which it appears to have lost amidst the troubles of recent years. The Turks have often been leaders in the Middle East—in Islamic empire under the Ottomans, in nationalist self-liberation under Kemal Atatürk, in responsible parliamentary government under his successors. Perhaps they will show the way again. There is no denying Turkey's troubles and the split between the secularists in the military and the Islamist government. In February of 2009, more than a dozen senior military officers were arrested on charges that they had been engaged in a plot to destabilize the government. By now it would seem that the government has obtained control of every part of the state except the judiciary—and that is under way.

In either case, what happens in Turkey will have immense and perhaps decisive effects in the region as a whole. A triumph of Islamic fundamentalism would probably spell the end of any hope of Islamic democracy for a long time. A fundamentalist Turkey might, for a while, maintain good relations with Iran, but sooner rather than later the historic pattern of the region would reappear. An Islamic Turkey and an Islamic Iran would again confront each other as rivals for leadership, the choice this time, as it was centuries ago, being between the Sunni and Shi'a versions of the faith.

In the meantime the fundamentalist movements pursue their distinctive patterns of action—terror at home while in opposition, repression at home and terror abroad when in power. Slitting the throats of harmless villagers in Algeria, bombing parties of uninvolved tourists who are the guests of Egypt, blowing up hotels in Amman—these have become the specific tactics of the movements that we have come to call Islamic fundamentalism. Terror against civilians has become their trademark.

But what do they have to do with Islam? The Qur'ān states not once but several times that "No man shall bear another's burden," that is to say that no one should be punished for the misdeeds of another. Islamic law permits hostages only in a reciprocal voluntary exchange as pledges for the fulfillment of an agreement. The Islamic laws of war prescribe good treatment for women, children and other noncombatants—"Do not attack them unless they first attack you." Yet the so-called Islamic fundamentalists seize hostages by force and sometimes torture and kill them and carry out random massacres of villagers, passengers, tourists and mere passersby with bombs, guns and kitchen knives.

Some Muslims are already beginning to ask whether the effect of fundamentalist activities is to uphold and defend Islam or discredit and undermine it. The mindless, ruthless, callous violence of so many fundamentalist actions may well strengthen these doubts.

The struggle between democracy and militant fundamentalism is not limited to the Arab and Islamic world. It is becoming increasingly important in Israel.

Religion as such has always played an important part in Israeli life. It is, after all, the core of Jewish identity and therefore also of Israeli statehood. What is new in the situation is not the role of religion as such—this goes back for millennia—but the new religio-political ideology, which is gaining increasing support among Israeli Jews and is already a powerful—at times divisive—factor in Israeli domestic politics.

Without the threat of major war from outside, the Israelis will be free to concentrate on their own internal problems and, more specifically, on their own internal differences. In the past, these were along more or less European lines— between a socialist left, a conservative right and a liberal center. There are signs that this is changing and that the fault line in Israeli politics in the coming years will be less European and more Middle Eastern. This means that the major confrontation will not be between right and left in the conventional Western sense of these terms, but between secular democracy and religious ideology.

The establishment and flourishing of democracy in Israel in the 60-odd years since the foundation of the state are in themselves astonishing. At first sight, there would seem to be every reason why democracy should fail in this country and in this situation. The vast majority of the inhabitants in Israel originated in countries with little or no democratic experience or tradition. The virtually continuous state of war and the consequent importance of the army and its commanders might easily have led to a military regime—the more so in a region where such regimes are normal. To make matters worse, the Israelis saddled themselves from the start with what must be one of the worst electoral systems in the free world and then, by the direct election of the prime minister, found a way of making it even worse. Fortunately, they have since repealed this "reform."

Nevertheless, democracy has survived and even flourished. Because of its enforced isolation from the region in which it is situated, Israel has, for most practical purposes, been part of the Western world, and its democracy functioned naturally in a predominantly Western international environment. For most Israelis, Washington, London, Paris or Rome were nearer than Damascus, Baghdad or Cairo.

But this situation is changing and Israel is becoming, much more than in the past, a part of the Middle East. To some extent, this is due to the increasing proportion of Jews of Middle Eastern origin in the population and therefore in the government of Israel; to a much greater extent, this is due to the increasing network of relations with Middle Eastern countries. Middle Eastern influences are already perceptible in many aspects of Israeli life. They are likely to continue and expand. In this respect, the peace process may bring a threat to Western-style democracy in Israel; it may also give much needed encouragement to the development of democracy in Middle Eastern countries. For example, the Arab League's permanent commission on human rights, founded in 1968, has hitherto concerned itself exclusively with the human rights of Palestinians under Israeli rule. It may now follow the example of the Organization of American States and the Organization of African Unity, with which it shares several members, and look at human rights in member states. There are already active groups in several Arab countries—or in exile—concerned with this issue. They will surely grow in numbers and in influence.

In Israel as in the Muslim lands, the threat to democracy does not come from religion as such, but from a religiously expressed ideology imbuing old terms with new meanings and using—or misusing—the faith and hope of the devout in order to gain and retain power. Faith and piety are perfectly compatible with an open, democratic society. State-enforced holy law administered by self-styled holy men is not.

War and Peace

Parliamentary politics, like that other great English invention, football, is a method by which rival parties can struggle for victory without violent conflict. Both sides in the struggle observe the same rules and share certain common principles. Both accept either victory or defeat with grace, because both know that victory can never be total nor defeat final. And just as conflicts of interest and policy between rival parties in a democracy can be conducted peacefully, so, too, can conflicts of interest and purpose between democratic states be pursued without resorting to war.

The position is different when the contending forces are defined, not by politics, not by economics, but by religion. For the old-style religious believer—there is some change among some modern believers—the conflict is not between rival beliefs, rival truths or rival interests; it is between truth and falsehood, and the upholders of falsehood have no rights in the present and no hope for the future. The unequivocal duty of the upholders of truth is to gain power and use it to promote and enforce that truth.

Even the nonreligious may admit the value of religion in moral, cultural and, above all, personal life. But many, even of the pious, are compelled to recognize the dangers of religion organized as a political force. In the fledgling or embryonic democracies of the Middle East, where cooperation in conflict is still a new and little-known concept, religious parties tend to become fundamentalist, and fundamentalism, by its very nature, is ruthless and uncompromising. Opposing democratic parties may cooperate within the state, rival democratic states may cooperate even in their international disagreements, but for fundamentalists there is no compromise, and dealings between rival contenders fall naturally and inevitably into the familiar forms of jihad and crusade.

How would this affect relations between Israel and its neighbors? Democracies may negotiate and compromise with other democracies. For religions, this is much more difficult and, for fundamentalist religions, impossible. Democratic Turkey was, until quite recently, Israel's closest partner in the region, with a steadily expanding range of commercial, political, cultural and military relations; fundamentalist Iran is the most implacable opponent of the peace process and will remain so unless and until there is a change of direction in Iran itself.

The Arab-Israel peace process began, not because of a change of heart on either side, but because of a change of circumstance—exhaustion and the realization that the wars in which they were engaged were unwinnable. Israel is no longer the state created by its founders, a pioneer society, rough and tough in its ways, austere and dedicated in its beliefs. It is becoming an affluent and liberal society, still patriotic but less willing to pay the costs and endure the hardships of maintaining an occupation over unwilling subjects. The Intifada brought this home. After a long struggle, the Israelis succeeded in containing it, but it became clear that they could only maintain their authority, if at all, at an unacceptable cost, both moral and material, and with an unacceptable transformation of the very nature of Israeli society.

On the Palestinian side, too, there was a growing realization that their war aims were unattainable by force of arms and that the continuation of armed struggle against Israel would entail increasing burdens for their own Palestinian people and command decreasing support among their Arab kinsfolk. The decisive change came after two major miscalculations by the Palestinian leadership. They had already made a major mistake by choosing the Axis in the Second World War. They compounded this error by choosing the Soviets in the Cold War and Saddam Hussein in the Gulf War. One may speculate how events would have evolved had the Cold War ended with the collapse of the United States. But it did not, and with the collapse of the Soviet Union, the Palestine Liberation Organization (PLO) found itself without a superpower patron. This loss was aggravated by Palestinian support for Saddam Hussein in the Gulf crisis and war in 1990–91. The loss of goodwill in the United States and among the other Western members of the coalition was comparatively unimportant. Much more serious was the loss of the goodwill of the Arab members of the anti-Saddam coalition—the Saudis, the Kuwaitis and the other Gulf states, who had been their strongest supporters and, more important, their paymasters in the struggle against Israel. They now became increasingly reluctant to pay and were even willing to think the unthinkable—a deal with Israel.

A peace process was thus inaugurated in the early 1990s between an isolated and weakened PLO seeking to salvage something from the ruins of their hopes and an affluent Israel ready to sacrifice some of its gains in order to achieve security for the remainder. A soldier-politician of stature,

Yitzhak Rabin, made Israel's call after his election in 1992. The Palestinian leader Yasser Arafat was brought into the West Bank and Gaza from his exile in Tunisia. Peace seemed possible, but Arafat came back unrehabilitated, and the years to come would show the folly of that choice.

Perhaps there was no alternative to Yasser Arafat; the leaders in the Palestinian territories had been too cowed to negotiate with Israel. The peace process born of this diplomacy would lurch from crisis to crisis. The Arab states gave it some cover but never fully embraced it. On balance, that diplomacy was better than the scenarios of confrontation offered by the radicals in the region. But the strategic environment was to be radically altered by a new Iranian push into the old conflict between Israel and the Arabs. The Iranians were keen to upstage the Arabs on a matter so central to the Arabs themselves. And the very balance of terror has been changed by Iran's pursuit of weapons of mass destruction. This is a threat that far outweighs Syria's menace, or the menace posed by Saddam Hussein while in power. Under the terms of the old standoff between Israel and the radical Arab states, a measure of deterrence held. To be sure, the Arab radicals desired the destruction of Israel but Israel's sophisticated weapons precluded a knock-out victory. The Iranian threat is of a different magnitude.

There is a radical difference between the Islamic Republic of Iran and other governments with nuclear weapons. This difference is expressed in what can only be described as the apocalyptic worldview of Iran's present rulers. This worldview and expectation, vividly expressed in speeches, articles and even schoolbooks, clearly shape the perception and therefore the policies of President Mahmoud Ahmadinejad and his disciples.

Even in the past it was clear that terrorists claiming to act in the name of Islam had no compunction in slaughtering large numbers of fellow Muslims. A notable example was the blowing up of the American embassies in East Africa in 1998, which killed a few American diplomats and a much larger number of uninvolved local passersby, many of them Muslims. There were numerous other Muslim victims in the various terrorist attacks of the last 15 years.

The phrase "Allah will know his own" is usually used to explain such apparently callous unconcern; it means that, while infidel, that is, non-Muslim, victims will go to a well-deserved punishment in hell, Muslims will be sent straight to heaven. According to this view, the bombers are in fact doing their Muslim victims a favor by giving them a quick pass to heaven and its delights—the rewards without the struggles of martyrdom. School textbooks tell young Iranians to be ready for a final global struggle against an evil enemy, named as the United States, and to prepare themselves for the privileges of martyrdom.

A direct attack on the United States, though possible, is less likely in the immediate future. Israel is a nearer and easier target, and Mr. Ahmadinejad has given indication of thinking along these lines. The Western observer would immediately think of two possible deterrents. The first is that an attack that wipes out Israel would almost certainly wipe out the Palestinians too. The second is that such an attack would evoke a devastating reprisal from Israel against Iran, since one may surely assume that the Israelis have made the necessary arrangements for a counterstrike even after a nuclear holocaust in Israel.

The first of these possible deterrents might well be of concern to the Palestinians—but not apparently to their fanatical champions in the Iranian government. The second deterrent—the threat of direct retaliation on Iran—is, as noted, already weakened by the suicide or martyrdom complex that plagues parts of the Islamic world today, and is without parallel in other religions or, for that matter, in the Islamic past. This complex has become even more important at the present day because of this new apocalyptic vision.

The moderate Arabs play a more conventional game and have opted for a cold peace with Israel. For many in the region, their caution is trumped by the radicalism of Iran and its bravado.

While the peace process could well continue because neither side can afford to abandon it, there is unlikely to be any increase in good will or friendly relations between Israel and the Arabs. If anything, the movement is in the opposite direction, as greater contact brings greater tension and more opportunity for mutual suspicion and resentment. Attempts to allay these suspicions have often served only to augment them. Deep Arab suspicion is likely to remain whatever government rules in Israel, though Israeli policies may increase or reduce it.

The literature available in Arabic about Israel and, more generally, about Jews, Judaism and Jewish history is overwhelmingly anti-Semitic, based largely on leftovers from the hate literature of the Third Reich. No correctives are available or, in most countries, permitted; even films in which Jews—individually or collectively—are portrayed in a sympathetic or favorable light are usually cut or banned. Arab soldiers and businessmen who have direct personal dealings with Israelis have a realistic appreciation of their human strengths and weaknesses. So too do a small and increasing group of statesmen. The academic establishment, the professions, and—most consistently and effectively— the media are, and will probably long remain, hostile. But there are already some bold spirits—poets and playwrights, philosophers and scientists—who dare seek dialogue and an end to struggle. If the peace process survives, there will surely be more. Among Palestinians there is a growing readiness to meet and even cooperate with Israeli colleagues. Elsewhere, and particularly in countries that have treaty relations with Israel and are therefore, as they see it, exposed to a threat of Israeli economic and cultural penetration, attitudes are, if anything, hardening. The few who think otherwise are fiercely denounced by their more obdurate compatriots.

This may change with the passage of time and a growth in self-confidence in the Arab world. Until then, the Israelis would be wise to concentrate on economic relations and to content themselves with the cessation of armed conflict and the development of the minimum structure of contact and communication between neighboring states that are at peace or, to be precise, not at war.

In time, resignation may grow into tolerance, tolerance to acceptance, acceptance to goodwill and even friendship. But this is clearly not imminent, and attempts to hasten the slow process of improvement might halt or even reverse it. The likeliest—and the best—prospect for the coming years is a cold peace in which Israel might expect minimal cooperation from the political and diplomatic establishment to avoid war. Businessmen may cooperate for mutual profit, soldiers out of mutual respect, politicians in recognition of a common enemy. But many intellectuals have none of these motives, and, with few but increasing exceptions, they will trail after the peace process rather than precede and advance it.

In an era when pan-Arab nationalism and the imperialisms against which it was directed have faded into an ever more remote past, the struggle against Israel remains the only common Arab cause, and only Israel's actions can from time to time revive the flagging fortunes of pan-Arabism. Some Israeli actions have already done more for the pan-Arab cause than any Arab leader since Gamal Abdel Nasser. Similarly, Israeli extremism, both nationalist and religious, is nourished and encouraged by the tendency of some Palestinian organizations to resort to bloody terrorism every time there is a hitch—or a success—in the negotiations.

The peace process still has a long way to go, on a path beset with obstacles and ambushes. It may be halted, deflected or even reversed by acts of folly or fanaticism or by the deadly combination of the two. Even the inexperience of new leaders may cause grave damage. These dangers may come from either side and may provoke a comparable response from the other. But as long as the international and regional circumstances which brought the parties to the negotiating table remain in effect, the peace process will continue, surviving both setbacks and crises. If the peace process has not yet achieved peace at a time when these circumstances no longer apply, then the prospects for Arabs and Israelis alike will be very dark.

In the long run the future of Arab-Israel relations will be determined by the outcome of the overarching regional struggle between democratic and fundamentalist ideologies, by the choices made by the peoples and their leaders. The triumph of democracy would eventually lead to a genuine and not merely formal peace. The triumph of militant fundamentalism on either side can only result in continuous and increasingly destructive struggle. The choice between democracy and fundamentalism will, of course, be profoundly influenced by the pace, or lack, of economic betterment. Democracy and tolerance come easier to the affluent than to the indigent.

The Arab-Israel conflict is not the only factor for war in the region. Other wars, though attracting less attention in the outside world, have lasted longer and caused more devastation. They could easily resume. An obvious starting point for a new war would be an act of aggression by one of the radical and militant regimes. One possibility is Syria, perhaps in the form of a quick, limited move to seize the Golan Heights. But the Syrian autocracy of Hafiz al-Asad and his son Bashaar is no match for Israel. In the Syrian scheme of things, primacy over Lebanon is of much greater importance than the restoration of the Golan Heights. Another possible objective, the incorporation of Jordan and Greater Palestine into Syria, would involve a full-scale war with Israel; this Syria's rulers would probably prefer to avoid. Similarly, the Syrian claim against Turkey for the lost province of Alexandretta would entail unacceptable risks. The Syrians, for all intents and purposes, have written off Alexandretta, and the border between Syria and Turkey has acquired a sense of permanence.

Inside Iran an almost classical situation for aggression and expansion prevails. An ageing and tiring revolutionary regime enjoys control of a vast network of terror in the region and beyond and of a powerful armory of conventional and, no doubt soon, unconventional weapons. The stress on nuclear development, in a country rich in oil and gas, can mean nothing else. The regime faces mounting discontent among ever larger sections of the population at home. The Iranian revolutionaries are in many ways following the path of their French and Russian predecessors—the struggle of radicals and pragmatists, the terror, the Thermidorian reaction. It is not impossible that the Iranian Revolution, too, may culminate in a Napoleon or a Stalin. They would be wise to remember that Napoleon's career ended at Waterloo and St. Helena and that Stalin's legacy to the Soviet Union was disintegration and chaos.

Revolutionary war is not the only threat to the Arab states. There is also the danger of old-fashioned territorial claims by more powerful neighbors—sometimes for part, sometimes for the whole, of the national territory. Syria has threatened the independence of both Jordan and Lebanon; for three decades (1976–2005), Syria's writ ran in Lebanon. It was the good fortune of the Lebanese that American power came to their rescue during a particularly assertive interlude in American diplomacy. Iraq has attempted by various means to make good its claims to Kuwait. It could do so again in the future, though the new Iraq that emerged out of the war of 2003 is unlikely to resume the adventurism of the prior dictatorship. Iran lays claim to the whole of Bahrain and has other unresolved territorial disputes in the Gulf area. It may develop claims on Persian-speaking Tajikistan and western Afghanistan. There are other smaller disputes on virtually all inter-Arab frontiers. Though these may for long periods be dormant, they can always be revived for immediate tactical or long-range strategic purposes.

One such is the Egyptian claim to the Sudan. At one time this claim, with the slogan "Unity of the Nile Valley," was a major theme of Egyptian nationalist ideology and later foreign policy. For some time now the claim has been tacitly abandoned, but it could easily be revived.

Perhaps the most artificial of all the Arab states is Libya, invented by the Italian ministry of colonial affairs in December 1932. Historically, Cyrenaica, the eastern half, was usually associated with Egypt; Tripolitania, the western half, with Tunisia. The frontier between Libya and Egypt was, after some disputes, resolved by negotiation between the masters of these two countries, Italy and Britain. Egyptians might well feel that they are not bound by such imperialist pacts. Some future Egyptian government, tired of the repeated failures of Egyptian policy in southwest Asia, might turn its attention to the more promising opportunities of Africa. Both Libya and the northern Sudan are tied to Egypt by bonds of religion, language, culture and history. The political structures in which they live are alien and artificial in origin and are deteriorating visibly in our time. Some form of union with Egypt might seem an acceptable solution to their, as well as to Egypt's, problems.

In recent years there have been several attempts, by free choice or by armed conquest, to merge two or more Arab states into some larger union. Almost all have failed. There may well be more attempts of both kinds, but their chances of survival are not great. There is of course one example of unity: the hegemony that Syria exercised in Lebanon. But this never had the consent of the Lebanese. It was a reign of political oppression and economic plunder. It harked back to the "fraternal" merger between the Soviet Union and its satellites. That grim Syrian chapter in Lebanon offers the Arabs, if anything, a cautionary tale as to the fate of the weak in the face of unchecked power.

CENTER AND PERIPHERY

Perhaps the greatest danger that threatens the Middle East is not wars between states but wars within states. The civil war in Lebanon is the most obvious example. The tragedies of Yugoslavia and Somalia, both on the edges of the Middle

East and sharing part of its history, are others. The continuing struggles in Sudan, according to an Egyptian estimate, have already killed five times as many people as all the Arab-Israel wars combined. But the outside world, including most of Africa, seems to view it with indifference. Sudan had little oil, no Jews, no holy places; it had no active well-wishers or even ill-wishers abroad. The recent discovery of oil may change all this.

For a time, Lebanon functioned smoothly as an open democracy—indeed the only such in the entire Arab world. But that democracy did not survive the importation of other peoples' problems and the intervention, first political then military, of other regional powers. Lebanese democracy foundered in a series of bloody civil wars. As the Lebanese state broke up, in the mid-1970s, loyalty to it become meaningless, and the country disintegrated into a patchwork of tribes, regions, sects and other interest groups, in unending conflict with each other and even within themselves. This anarchic fragmentation was ended only when Syria established effective military control over most of the country and political control over its government. The Syrians all but erased the border between the two countries. After three decades of brutal Syrian rule, the Lebanese appeared to lose sovereignty over their homeland. The American war in Iraq delivered the Lebanese their chance. Syria had done its best to thwart the American effort in Iraq, and the American response came in Syria's sphere of influence, in Lebanon. There was enough American power nearby to intimidate and worry the Syrians. In a moment of panic, in the spring of 2005, the Syrians gave up their dominion in Lebanon. To be sure, they were still next door, and their intelligence operatives and local quislings were still on the ground in Lebanon. But the blatant occupation had been dismantled.

Hafiz al-Asad had defied the odds and had bequeathed power to his son, but the regime in Damascus was still the rule of a sectarian minority, the Alawis. And it still had the weakness of its origins. The Syrian state was constructed after the First World War from the ruins of the Ottoman Empire. Its frontiers were defined and its identity determined by agreements between the British and French governments. For Arab nationalists, this state was a construct, a fragment of the greater Arab fatherland. For Syrian patriots, it was the rump of a greater Syria which included not only Lebanon but also Transjordan and Palestine. But for some of the peoples within its frontiers, even this smaller state with its capital in Damascus was too much. The Alawis of the northwest and the Druze of the southeast mounted serious rebellions against the central government, and secessionist tendencies also appeared in other regions of the north, the center and the south. The nationalist aim has always been to merge the state into some larger, vaguer entity. A more likely outcome will be the Lebanese paradigm—to dissolve the state and fragment its territories into rival feuding fiefdoms.

Iraq, another post–First World War construct, faces the same problems and the same dangers. Assembled from three provinces of the Ottoman Empire, the vilayets of

Mosul, Baghdad and Basra, it is divided ethnically between Arabs and Kurds, religiously between Sunnis and Shi'a, socially between townspeople, cultivators and nomads. When Saddam's regime faltered briefly in the aftermath of the Gulf War in 1991, all of these centrifugal tendencies came out into the open. While the victorious coalition looked on, he was able to crush these various dissident forces one by one. The American invasion in 2003, which shattered the tyranny of the Ba'ath Party and of Saddam Hussein, rewrote Iraq's history. Outside intervention by the preeminent Western power upended the Sunni ascendency and gave new power to the Shi'a in Baghdad and to the Kurds in their ancestral land in the north. Iraq's prospects are promising, but it remains to be seen if the Sunni Arabs will adjust to their loss of power and dominion.

It is not only imperialist constructs that face the danger of fragmentation. The Kingdom of Saudi Arabia, also a creation of the interwar period, was not the result of imperial expansion and compromise. It is a creation of dynastic ambition, tribal loyalty and religious zeal. At first sight, the Saudi kingdom would appear to be relatively homogeneous. There are no ethnic minorities, since all its people—apart from guest workers—are Arab. There are no religious minorities, since Islam is the only permitted religion. Yet there are difficulties. The Arabs are divided by region and more especially by tribe, with an ancient tradition of tribal feuding. The Muslims are divided into Sunni and Shi'a, the latter a minority in the Kingdom as a whole, but massively present in the eastern, oil-bearing provinces. Even the reigning dynasty is riven by factional, sectional and personal rivalries. Economic and social changes are creating new ambitions and new grievances. The vast ramshackle Kingdom has been held together principally by religion and money. Now, religion is becoming a divisive force, as fundamentalist movements denounce what they see as the impiety of the ruling house and the ruling class. Money, once plentiful enough to solve all problems, is now becoming less readily available. The development of both the religious mood and the oil market suggest that these problems will grow worse, not better, in the coming years.

The Kingdom faces no immediate threat of external aggression, at least not in the form of open warfare. And doubtless, the United States would be sure to come to the rescue of the Saudi realm in the face of outside aggression, as it did in 1990–91. But there is a growing danger of subversion at home, some, though by no means all of it, externally inspired. The House of Saud was challenged by zealots who opened a campaign of terror on Saudi soil in 2003. It was a tenacious fight. The regime prevailed, but the struggle revealed the vulnerability of the Wahhabi order to politico-religious sedition. Against this kind of threat, the magnificent armory of high-tech weapons imported from the United States offers no protection. The Israelis learnt during the Intifada that sophisticated weaponry against stone-throwing youths can be counterproductive. The other governments in the region are not subject to the same constraints, domestic and international, as are the Israelis, but they too show signs of learning the limits of repression.

Even the most advanced of missiles, even the deadliest of unconventional weapons of war can neither suppress nor deter rioters or terrorists. The latter may even find a use for them.

In one respect Saudi Arabia is better placed than Syria or Iraq; that is, in its enormous size. Most of the country consists of desert, and the centers of population are like islands in an archipelago, separated by vast expanses of emptiness. This makes it easier to contain, isolate, and eventually repress any outbreak of active opposition.

What is true of Saudi Arabia applies to a greater or lesser extent to the other oil states of the Persian Gulf. In some respects they are better situated than the Saudis; in others they are more dangerously exposed, in the immediate neighborhood of two more powerful neighbors, Iraq and Iran, and in desperate need of American protection.

The collapse and disintegration of any one of these states would create a dangerous situation in the region, especially for its neighbors—a threat to the fragile, a temptation to the strong. Here again the civil war in Lebanon and the involvement of its near and even its distant neighbors could serve as a paradigm for the region.

Not all Arab states face the danger of fragmentation. Some are sustained by long experience of stability and continuity and memories of at least local or regional autonomy. These have combined to produce a common identity, a sense of nationhood that is likely to survive the internal and external problems they may confront in the years to come. An obvious example is Egypt, a nation by any definition. In the future as in the past, it will remain distinctively Egyptian, whatever changes of regime or even of culture it may undergo. Another example is Morocco, which, like Egypt, was created by geography and history. Other countries whose past gives some hope for continuing nationhood and statehood are Tunisia, Yemen, and perhaps a reconstituted democratic Lebanon.

Though Arab states are the most endangered, they are not the only ones in peril. The trend towards fragmentation will be encouraged by the growth of ethnicity and sectarianism. The seductive idea of self-determination has spread to a number of ethnic minorities no longer satisfied with their previous status.

By far the most important of these are the Kurds, numbering many millions and speaking a language, or rather a group of interrelated dialects, of the same linguistic family as Persian. The Kurds are a very ancient people, but they never achieved separate statehood, and their homeland is divided among the modern states of Turkey, Iraq and Iran, in all of which they have played an important part. Smaller groups are also found in Syria and in the Transcaucasian republics.

Paradoxically, it was in Iraq that the Kurds were to achieve a great measure of autonomy over their own affairs. Foreign (read American) protection secured for the Kurds a zone of self-rule in northern Iraq. A binational Iraq, part Kurdish and part Arab, emerged out of the American war of 2003. The Kurds developed the military ability and political skills to guard the measure of federalism enshrined in

Iraq's new constitution. Inevitably, this upsurge of Kurdish nationalism in Iraq was to be felt, most intensely, in Turkey. The struggle in Turkey has been very bitter—armed insurrection and terror on the one side, harsh repression on the other. But there are signs of improvement. There have never been any obstacles to the advancement of Kurds in Turkey, even to the highest offices in the land, but always on condition of a total acceptance of Turkish identity and the renunciation of any Kurdish identity. Even the Kurdish language was proscribed.

This is no longer true. Kurdish is freely and widely used, and Kurdish books are on sale in the bookshops even of Ankara and Istanbul. There is also a change on the Kurdish side. Turkey's Kurds show realism in their ambitions and an ability to play the political game by the norms and ways of democracy. One may hope, during the coming years, to see the beginnings of a compromise between Turks and Kurds. This would not involve a Kurdish state, against which all three powers would be adamantly opposed. It could, however, include a significant measure of cultural and perhaps some regional autonomy, making it possible for Kurds to cherish and develop their Kurdish cultural identity while being loyal and productive citizens of the Turkish Republic. Some kind of arrangement along the lines of the coexistence of English, Scots and Welsh in the United Kingdom could provide the answer. It may be noted in passing that a Turkish statesman asked to comment on this suggestion replied: "The Kurds aren't Scotch; they're Irish."

The future of the Kurdish minority in Iran offers much less hope at the present time and is clearly bound up with the very problematic future course of events in that country. Iran is threatened by centrifugal forces: the Persians properly so called form a bare majority of the total population. The rest belong to other ethnic groups and speak other languages. A potentially dangerous feature is that, on many of the frontiers of Iran, the inhabitants share a language and an identity with the people on the other side. In the northwest, the Iranian province of Azerbaijan adjoins the independent former Soviet republic of the same name. In the southwest, the province of Khuzistan is inhabited by Arabic speakers very similar to those of Iraq. In the southeast, the people of Iranian Baluchistan share a common identity with the Baluchis of Afghanistan and Pakistan. Along the eastern and northeastern frontiers, speakers of various Turkic and Iranic languages share a cultural and—perhaps more dangerous—religious, Sunni identity with their neighbors in Afghanistan and in Central Asia. Hitherto they have been held together by Iranian patriotism—by a shared sense of historic identity. But it is easy to imagine a situation in which the central government in Tehran becomes too weak or too oppressive—either could lead to the other—to retain the loyalty of the frontier provinces. And in such a case, Iran, too, could follow the Lebanese paradigm.

The danger in Iran, however, is not as great as in Syria, Iraq or Saudi Arabia. Unlike these, Iran is not a new state, nor is it of Western manufacture. It is an old state with centuries, indeed millennia, of sovereign existence and a strong sense of cultural identity which in the past has usually served to counterbalance and, in the last analysis, to outweigh the centrifugal forces of regionalism and factionalism. This happened in 1926 when a determined and ambitious young officer, seeing his country falling apart under an incompetent ruler, saved the unity of the nation by seizing power and establishing a new dynasty. It could happen again. For now, the mullahs have the upper hand, but, as the upheaval in the summer of 2009—three decades after the triumph of the theocracy—was to show, the struggle over Iran's identity and future is far from settled. On the borders of Iran, in both Afghanistan and Iraq, American military intervention gave rise to new regimes. At the time of the American invasion of Iraq, an Iranian complained: "You should have tackled your problems in alphabetical order." An Iranian joke current during the campaign in Afghanistan related that many Iranians put signs on top of their houses, in English, with the text: "This way please!" The American military push into the region bypassed Iran, and its rulers—or people—were left free to make their own history and to navigate their own course.

OIL AND WATER

Today, with the ending, at least for the time being, of global strategic confrontation, the most important single element in the Middle East, for the outside world, is oil. Middle

Eastern countries, now including the former Soviet republics in Transcaucasia and Central Asia, contain the largest proven resources of oil in the whole world, and more are being discovered all the time. But there is growing dissatisfaction with a fuel that pollutes the land, the sea and the air wherever it is used or transported and makes the world economy heavily dependent on the whims of such rulers as Hugo Chavez of Venezuela and Mahmoud Ahmadinejad of Iran. The kings and princes of Arabia are better trading partners than any of these, but continuing uncertainties about their future policies or even, in some cases, their survival make dependence on them uncomfortable.

For environmental and political as well as economic reasons, a continuous search has been in progress, first, for sources of oil other than the Middle East, and second, more important, sources of energy other than oil. In time, the advance of science and technology, which made oil first useful and then necessary, will make it obsolete, and replace it with cleaner, cheaper and more accessible sources of energy. The exploitation of natural gas may delay but will not prevent this ending. When it happens, those who depend on oil revenues will face a new and bleak reality, and the outside world will no doubt view the struggles and upheavals of the Middle East with the same calm detachment—or as some might put it, callous indifference—with which it now views the civil wars in Somalia and Liberia. Until then, the consumer countries—Europe and the Far East far more than the United States—will be anxiously dependent on whoever rules the oil wells and will have to devise and apply their policies accordingly. It will be neither a safe nor an easy task.

For the time being, oil remains the major, for some indeed the only, resource. In the oil-producing countries it provides most or all of their foreign currency earnings. Even in the Middle Eastern countries with little or no oil, there is a ripple effect, in the form of subsidies of one sort or another, labor migration, and, to a surprisingly limited extent, investment.

This overwhelming dependence on the export of irreplaceable and nonrenewable natural resources is obviously dangerous, and when these resources are exhausted or superseded, it will become catastrophic. Reserves of nonrenewable resources are already falling rapidly, and even renewable resources like water are used at unsustainably high levels. These exceed 100 percent in Israel, Jordan, the Palestine territories, Libya and virtually the whole of the Arabian peninsula. In addition, the loss from land degradation is currently estimated to cost 11.5 billion dollars a year.

The oil states will face two crises, the first from exhaustion, the second from supersession. A few countries—Iraq, Saudi Arabia and the Transcaucasian and Central Asian republics—still have vast unexploited resources that could last into an indefinite future. The rest, notably Iran, are less well placed. In the course of the twenty-first century, they will find themselves bereft of what has become their main resource. In the Gulf states, from a global or even a regional perspective, this would be of relatively minor importance. The guest workers will return whence they came or go elsewhere; the states, with their very small populations, will return to the obscurity from which they briefly emerged. But Iran is another matter—a large area with a rapidly growing population, a powerful state supported, on the one hand, by a militant revolutionary ideology and, on the other, by an increasingly efficient machine of war. As the revolution approaches its Napoleonic or Stalinist phase, and as the oil resources of Iran approach exhaustion, the rulers of that country, whoever they may be at that time, will inevitably look toward the still vast resources of their neighbors.

The best prospect for the region would of course be a regional program of cooperation and development. The past record of the region and the character and habits of most of its present rulers make a bitter struggle much more probable.

In such a situation, those countries that have learnt to live and advance without oil revenues, such as Turkey, Jordan, Israel, Tunisia and Morocco, will be at a considerable advantage.

Figures for growth in incomes, exports, job creation, and school enrollment vary greatly in the region. Israel, with its relatively well-educated population and its high-tech industries, leads easily. It is followed by Turkey, with an upsurge of private enterprise in both domestic production and export trade. Some flourishing regional developments have even given rise to the phrase "Anatolian tigers," implying comparison with the soaring economies of East Asia. Of the Arab countries, Morocco, Tunisia and Jordan have the best records and show the greatest promise. Morocco and Tunisia have low military expenditure; that of Jordan is being reduced. All three, lacking exportable natural resources, rely heavily on human resource development. This is reflected in the figures for literacy and school enrollment, infant mortality and life expectancy. Tunisia has made notable progress in bringing education, from primary to university level, to its female population and enabling increasing numbers of women to play a significant part in public life

Most of the region lags behind other regions in exports, in private investment, in productivity, and in the efficient management of natural resources. Many have failed to improve or even maintain the already low living standards of their populations. Real exports per capita show an overall decline. This will worsen if, as some predict, oil prices remain flat or, at best, uncertain.

An even greater issue than oil—since it directly affects not just some but all the states of the region—will be water. The agriculture of the Middle East is no longer sufficient to feed its people, and the disparity will become worse. A rapidly growing population constantly requires more food. The need to house them and the consequent spread of villages and towns reduces the capacity to produce it.

Agriculture depends on soil and water. The Middle East lacks the great and fertile plains of other more fortunate regions of the world. Most of its surface consists of mountains and deserts with only limited areas of cultivated land dependent on rivers. Rivers present both technical and political problems.

The technical problems can, to a limited extent, be overcome by dams and irrigation schemes. The political problems, hitherto quiescent, will be aggravated by this kind of construction. The sources of many of the great rivers on which Middle Eastern countries depend lie in other regions not subject to their control. The headwaters of the river Jordan, vital to Israel and Palestine and Jordan, are in Syria. The headwaters of the Euphrates, lifeblood of Syria and still more of Iraq, are in Turkey. The Nile passes several frontiers in its long journey from its sources to Egypt.

In the past, this was not of great importance. It is now and will be more so as population growth creates an increasing demand for water, and technology an increasing capacity to control it. In the course of time, oil and gas may be exhausted or superseded. Water may be exhausted, but it will never be superseded, and in a not-too-distant future, water will become the outstanding issue between the nations of the region, exacerbating enmities and straining friendships.

Here, even more than with oil, there is a choice between conflict and cooperation. Turkey, the only country in the region with an exportable surplus of water, has from time to time offered to export it through pipelines or by sea. Such schemes came to nothing because of conflict and mistrust between the nations through which such pipelines would pass. In a peaceful Middle East, with a structure of regional cooperation, such schemes could be revived. More important, the countries might cooperate in projects of desalination. For the time being at least, this is the only answer to the water problems of the region. The waters of the sea are inexhaustible and could provide for all needs to an indefinite future. Desalination plants are already functioning in some places, but there are problems, two in particular. The first is that, with present technology and under present conditions, desalination is for most countries economically unworkable. The second is that desalination plants are dangerously vulnerable to attack, whether by terrorism or by conventional arms.

In the meantime, some interim measures can and probably will be adopted to secure a more economic use of existing water resources. Growing wheat in Saudi Arabia and vegetables and fruit in the desert emirates may have a certain dramatic value, but it is a wasteful misuse of water and will no doubt be abandoned when good sense prevails over display. A less obvious but nevertheless significant saving could be achieved by abandoning the growing of such water-intensive and nonessential crops as bananas. Even the great Israeli standby, the orange, will give way to other crops more suited to an arid climate. Significant experiments in desert and semidesert agriculture are already being pursued at research centers in Israel. These could serve as pilot projects for the whole region.

The economic crisis of the region is acute by any measure. To begin with, there is the unhealthy role of the state in economic life. According to the Arab Human Development Report 2009 (the fifth in a series, published by the United Nations Development Program [UNDP]), government revenues as percentage of GDP are 13 percent in the

Third World countries, but they are 25 percent in the Middle East and North Africa. The oil states are particularly given to state domination of the economy: the comparable figures are 68 percent in Libya, 45 percent in Saudi Arabia and 40 percent in Algeria, Kuwait and Qatar. The unemployment rates for the Arab world are the highest in the world, and the UNDP report estimates that 51 million jobs are needed by 2020 to "absorb young entrants to the labor force who otherwise face an empty future." Despite all the oil in the region, tens of millions of Arabs are living below the poverty lines. Demography compounds the misery. The population of the Arab world is expected to grow some 40 percent over the next two decades.

A few years ago, it came to light that the total exports other than fossil fuels of the Arab world plus Iran amount to less than those of Finland. As the region becomes ever more dependent on food imports, there will be greater need for manufactured exports. A continuing problem is the lag in investment because of burdensome regulations, low privatization, poor and often deteriorating infrastructure, and underdeveloped financial markets. Far from attracting outside investment to the region, wealthy Middle Easterners tend to invest much of their money elsewhere. Conflict and insecurity could only aggravate these trends.

Of all the Arab countries, the ones with the best economic records are Morocco, Tunisia, and Jordan. All three function without the oil revenues that have distorted the growth of Saudi Arabia and the Gulf States. All three have avoided the disastrous statist policies that still encumber the economies of Algeria and Egypt. All three devote major resources to education and infrastructure. Tunisia in particular spends more than any other Muslim country on female education. All three have rapidly improving health conditions—including lower infant mortality and greater life expectations. These developments show very clearly the way to greater prosperity through peace to peaceful development. Syria and Iraq under the long rule of their Ba'ath parties showed with at least equal clarity the way to disaster through political and economic tyranny and domestic and foreign conflict. There can be little doubt which of these paths the people of Syria and Iraq would have chosen—if ever they were able to exercise a choice. Iraq was given a chance in 2003; its prospects look promising, but the weight of the past and the curse of oil (the easy money in the coffers of the state) weigh heavily on the new order.

The population explosion in the Middle East and North Africa is already producing another important phenomenon—migration of labor. Western Europe has, and in the not too distant future, Central and Eastern Europe will have, a relatively high standard of living and a low birth rate. Their southern and southeastern neighbors in North Africa and the Middle East share a low standard of living and a high birth rate. Modern travel and political relaxation make it easier both to reach and enter the various countries of Europe. Already the migration of labor, especially from Turkey and North Africa to Western Europe, is seen by many in these countries as a major problem. The peace process between Israel and its Arab neighbors, if it continues, may well produce similar results, as Palestinian and perhaps also other Arab labor is attracted to the expanding Israeli economy.

A significant element in the cash flow of the region is aid and donations of various kinds. By far the most important single source is the government of the United States, which provides a wide range of financial aid for both development and military purposes. The principal recipients are Israel, Egypt and Jordan, followed by Turkey and Armenia. (Further afield, Pakistan and Afghanistan have become big magnets for American military and economic assistance.) Given the burdens of the American economy—huge budget deficits, a growing public debt—this aid is unlikely to continue in its present form. Military aid will dwindle as the danger of a military confrontation recedes. Economic aid will be seen as unnecessary where it is effective and useless where it is not. In Israel, where the military danger shows little sign of receding, military aid will probably continue. Economic aid will be more difficult to justify, as its place in the rapidly developing and increasingly sophisticated Israeli economy becomes less important. Aid to Egypt passes through the United States Congress on the coattails of aid to Israel and would probably not make it on its own—the more so at a time when Egyptian policy towards the American-sponsored peace process is seen as equivocal.

Considerable sums also come from abroad in the form of private donations, mainly from Jewish and Muslim communities in the Americas, Western Europe and Australasia. Most of this money is designated for development, education, welfare and other charitable purposes; some of it is diverted to overtly or covertly political aims. The distinction is not always easy to discern or maintain. Terrorist and subversive movements of various kinds, some of them state sponsored, are finding in Europe and North America a freedom of maneuver, both financial and operational, which they could not hope to find in the Middle East or North Africa.

They are using this freedom to devastating effect. The Iranian Revolution against the Shah took an enormous step forward when its leader Khomeini moved from Iraq to Paris, where he had uncensored modern communications at his disposal. Others are following and will follow this early successful example. Among the Turkish diaspora in Europe, especially in Germany, both the fundamentalists and the Kurdish separatists collect funds and organize subversion. To an alarming extent the internal struggle in Algeria is planned, financed and directed from France. The Iranian government's "Office of Islamic Revivals," concerned with the promotion of the Islamic revolution and its ideas in other Muslim countries, also locates its main financial and operational basis in Europe. At the same time the Islamic republic is itself threatened by increasingly sophisticated opposition groups using Western democratic freedom and modern communication to challenge the regime at home.

There are also transfers of funds within the region, some from governments, notably Iran and Libya, some from wealthy private individuals, mostly in Saudi Arabia and the

Gulf. In Turkey, the only Muslim country in the region with free and contested elections, these transfers take the form of suitably disguised campaign contributions. Even in the older and more experienced democracies of the West, such contributions and their effect are difficult to follow and document. Their effect will be far greater in the newer democracies of poorer countries, with less experience in following the trail of money and measuring its impact. These tasks will however become easier as the flow of oil money diminishes and the democracies of the region become more experienced in detection and counteraction.

Tourism has been described as one of the best prospects for the region. Certainly there is room for improvement—at the present time the tourist revenues of the entire region are less than those of Mexico and about equal to those of Thailand in the 1990s. But the development of tourism, as of so much else, will depend on domestic and regional security. Great numbers of tourists are not likely to brave the dangers of war and terrorism.

With a few exceptions, the economic prognosis for the region remains bad. Productivity is falling dramatically, the creation of new jobs has stagnated, unemployment rates are the highest in the world. The poor are becoming more numerous and, comparatively, poorer. Major economic development will be needed to avoid disaster, and this in turn will presuppose the social, cultural and scientific changes needed to bring the Middle East into line with the developed countries of both West and East.

PAST AND FUTURE

The competition between democracy and fundamentalism will have a direct bearing on another choice—between outward and inward modernization. Outward modernization means accepting the devices, the amenities, the conveniences provided by Western science and industry while rejecting what are seen as pernicious Western values. All too often, this means also rejecting the science that produced these devices and amenities and the way of life that made that science possible. One might put it this way: outward modernization means buying and firing a gun; inward modernization means learning to manufacture and ultimately design one. This is not likely to happen in countries—like some in the region—where science is taught in schools from 50-year-old textbooks.

Catching up with the modern world means more than borrowing or buying modern technology. It means becoming part of the process by which that technology is created—that is, undergoing the intellectual revolution, the economic, social and eventually political transformation that precede, accompany and follow technological change.

In this respect, the Middle East still lags far behind other more recent recruits to modernity such as Korea, Taiwan and Singapore. It lags much further behind Japan, whose first contact with the West came centuries later than that of the Middle East. The transformation of the "Asian tigers" is even more dramatic, and the gap between them and the

economies of the Middle East is widening every day. In a
region where hundreds of universities turn out tens of
thousands of engineers every year, it has become normal for
governments and corporations requiring high-tech construction work to bring in contractors from Korea—a
country that only recently emerged from a long period of
oppressive colonial rule followed by devastating years of
war. Unless the countries of the Middle East are able to
make the transition to the new age, this gap will grow ever
wider.

There are three factors which could help transform the
Middle East: Turkey, Israel and women—the first previously aloof, the second previously excluded, the third previously suppressed.

Of these, the most important is women. They will, if permitted, play a major role in bringing the Middle East into a
new era of material development, scientific advancement
and sociopolitical liberation. Of all the people of the Middle
East, women have the strongest vested interest in social and
political freedom. They are already among freedom's most
valiant and effective defenders; they may yet be the region's
salvation. As in other parts of the world, some women
defend and even acclaim the subordination of their sex.
Others, never having known anything else, meekly submit
to it. But growing numbers, touched by the ideas of freedom and equality and increasingly open to outside influence and example, will rebel against it. Muslim countries
cannot hope to catch up, let alone keep pace, with the
advanced world, as long as they deprive themselves of the

talents and energies of half the population and entrust the early nurture of most of the other half to uneducated and downtrodden mothers.

The women's movement will still suffer serious reverses in the Middle East. But these, like the excesses of the Taliban in Afghanistan and the murderous repression of women in some Arab countries, will not succeed indefinitely. Even in Iran, where antifeminism was a major theme in Khomeinist ideology, women are already beginning to play an increasing part in some aspects of public life. The influence of women from among the expatriate Muslim communities in Europe and America will also make an important contribution to the emancipation of their sisters who stayed at home.

Turkey today stands before important choices. It may choose, as some of its leaders would clearly prefer, to turn its back on the West and return to the Middle East, this time not leading but following, in a direction determined by others. This would appear to be the preferred choice of the Justice and Development Party that came to power in 2002 and strengthened its position five years later when it claimed the presidency for one of its own. It may choose, as other Turkish leaders would clearly prefer, to tighten its ties with the West and turn its back on the Middle East, except for those countries that share Turkey's westward orientation and democratic aspirations. In either case, Turkey can and probably will play a growing role in the region. The Turks have greater political experience, a more developed economy, and a more balanced society than the Arab states.

The Turkish example, perhaps even Turkish leadership, may play a crucial role in influencing Arab choices. The decisions made in Turkey in the near future will determine in which direction Turkish influence will point. An Islamist Turkey is bound to tip the balance in favor of the theocratic model of government. This would be a huge setback for Turkey's modernism and for the prospects of modernity in the Arab states as well.

The Arab-Israel conflict, too, in one way or another, will profoundly influence the development of the region as a whole. This could be positive or negative. If the struggle becomes more bitter and acquires the enduring quality of some of the other, more ancient quarrels of the region, it will have a corrosive effect on both Israeli and Arab societies, diverting energies and resources from creative to destructive purposes and preventing the progress of the region toward a new age of advanced technology and political freedom.

Peace, in contrast, would help and speed that progress. Even the negative aspects of Israeli rule may unintentionally contribute, in some respect and in some degree, to this process. Almost every day, radio and television—including, especially, Israeli radio and television—report on Palestinian protests against Israeli repression, in parliament, in the courts, in the media, and in the street, where demonstrators gather to vent their anger. It will not escape notice that all this is an innovation in a region where normally citizens do not sue the government in the courts and critics do not denounce the policies they dislike in parliament and in the state-run media. Even more important, in most of these countries youths do not throw stones at soldiers, and the latter do not respond to attack with water cannon and rubber bullets. These differences are being seen and understood.

If there is peace, then the peoples of the Middle East, working together, might achieve their own breakthrough as other regions have already done and resume the creative role which they once played in the history of civilization. One way that this might happen was described in a remarkably prophetic article, entitled "The Changing East," by T. E. Lawrence—Lawrence of Arabia—published in 1920: "The success of [the Zionists'] scheme will involve inevitably the raising of the present Arab population to their own material level, only a little after themselves in point of time, and the consequences might be at the highest importance for the future of the Arab world. It might well prove a source of technical supply rendering them independent of industrial Europe, and in that case the new confederation might become a formidable element of world power. However, such a contingency will not be for the first or even the second generation."

With peace and cooperation between the nations of the region, it might be possible to resolve many problems and inaugurate a great economic expansion. In this, Israel, with its advanced and sophisticated technological and scientific base, would be able to make a substantial contribution.

Such cooperation would require the overcoming of many psychological barriers—the allaying of mistrust, the forgetting of grievances, the swallowing of pride. All these are difficult, perhaps impossible, but without them the region has little hope of moral or material advancement.

In the 1990s the combined G.N.P. of Egypt, Jordan, Syria and Lebanon, that is, all Israel's Arab neighbors, was significantly smaller than that of Israel alone. The per capita discrepancy is even greater. The most recent figures, for the year 2009, show some comparative change. But Israel's per capita G.N.P. is still 3.8 times that of Lebanon, 7.5 times that of Jordan, 9 times that of Syria, and 13.7 times that of Egypt. Cooperation could lead to the fulfillment of Lawrence's prophecy and narrow the gap between Israel and her Arab neighbors. A continuation of conflicts and boycotts would surely widen the gap.

A realist would argue, with reasonable certainty, that the odds against an Israeli-Palestinian settlement are discouragingly long. Dictatorships that rule much of the Middle East today will not, indeed cannot, make peace, because they need conflict to justify their tyrannical oppression of their own people and to deflect their peoples' anger against an external enemy. As with the Axis powers and the Soviet Union, real peace will come only with their defeat, or preferably collapse, and their replacement by governments that have been chosen, and can be dismissed, by their people and that will seek to resolve, not provoke, conflicts. At best, the dictatorships that have made the Israeli-Palestinian conflict their cause and their alibi for political and economic decay would countenance an armed peace. It would be wishful thinking to bet on economic and political progress in the shadow of this kind of uncertainty.

A RETURN TO EMPIRE?

This window of opportunity will not remain open forever. Even when its oil and its transit routes, so crucial in the past, are outdated by modern technology and communications, the Middle East will still be important—as the junction of three continents, the center of three religions, a strategic asset or danger to be coveted or feared. Sooner or later it will again become an object of interest to outside powers—old powers reviving, new powers emerging. If it continues on its present course, the region, lacking the capacities of India and China, on the one side, or the technology of Europe and America, on the other, will once again be a stake rather than a player in the great game of international politics.

For the moment, the peoples or governments of the Middle East can to an increasing extent determine their own fate. They may choose the way of Yugoslavia or Lebanon, of fragmentation and endless internecine strife. They may launch—there are some who clearly desire this—a new holy war, a jihad, which could again provoke, as it did a thousand years ago, the response of an opposing holy war, a crusade. A militant movement or power that defines itself in religious terms will also define its opponents in religious terms, and these opponents may sooner or later accept that definition. The so-called Islamic fundamentalists fight for Islam and explicitly reject the notion of patriotic or national loyalties, which they see as pagan, divisive and—worst of all—the result of Western influence. And since their cause is Islam, their enemies are those whom they see as the enemies of Islam—the followers of other religions or of none. Among nationalists and patriots the struggle was waged against Zionism and imperialism. In the language of the fundamentalists, these have resumed their earlier names— the Jews and the Christians. No one has a better claim to be called "Egyptian" than the Copts, the native Christians of Egypt. But attacks on Coptic churches and villages have become a common tactic of the Islamic fundamentalists, acting not in the name of country, but of the faith. Struggles of this kind can only exacerbate relations between the Middle East and the outside world and increase the possibility of a return to empire.

As long as conflict and repression prevail, there is little hope of the Middle East achieving a real equality with more advanced countries and therefore of preserving its independence from them. When vibrant and torpid, stronger and weaker, societies live side by side, some form of penetration and perhaps even of domination becomes inevitable.

Who would be the players in such a renewed game of great power politics in the Middle East? The United States has clearly demonstrated its lack of imperial ambition, at least in this region. Even when American power is pulled in by chaos, the Americans do not stay long. Important

American economic interests remain, and their protection at times requires a military presence, usually at the solicitation of local rulers. But these two interests will dwindle when the oil era draws to its inevitable end. Apart from some promising developments of high-tech industry—on a small scale and in a few places—there is little else in the Middle East to attract the attention of either investors or predators. The total amount of American private investment in the whole Middle East is about one-third of the amount invested in Australia, one-fifth of the amount invested in Japan and less than one-tenth of the amount invested in Canada. These disparities have been increasing for a number of years and are likely to become greater in the years to come.

America's major strategic interest ended with the Cold War. Terrorism, and the engagements in Afghanistan and Iraq, gave rise to a new American concern with the region. As of this writing, American forces are on the ground in Arab and Muslim states as never before. But by all indications, the American public bristles at this new engagement and yearns to leave that arc of discord to deal with its own troubles.

The European powers, singly or jointly, are unlikely to return to the scenes of their former imperial failures. The crises in Bosnia and Cyprus demonstrated their inability to cope unaided even with problems on their own doorstep. More probably they will content themselves with financial and commercial dealings, with perhaps a little occasional political profit taking when opportunity offers. There will be no European answer to Iran's nuclear drive, and Europe can be expected to avert its gaze from the misdeeds of Middle Eastern tyrannies.

Russia is another matter. For the moment Russia, crippled by its internal problems, is out of the game, and its weakness is painfully revealed in the few unsuccessful attempts by Russian leaders to assert a role in the peacemaking process. But there can be no doubt that at some time in the near or distant future this will change. A country with the resources and numbers and the scientific and technological sophistication of Russia will not indefinitely remain on the sidelines. Sooner or later Russia will be back, and we do not know what kind of a Russia it will be. It may fall subject to some form of totalitarian tyranny, fascist or communist; it may resume its earlier role as the leader of pan-Slavism or of Orthodox Christianity; it may succeed, after so many failed efforts, in establishing a Russian liberal democracy. It may resume or reject its former imperial ambitions. But this much can be said with certainty—that whatever kind of regime rules in a resurgent Russia, it will be vitally concerned with the Middle East—a region not far from its southern frontier, wherever that may ultimately lie, and linked by ties of history, religion and culture with important elements of the Russian population, including both Jews and Muslims as well as Christians.

The rulers of a new Russia would have several choices of Middle Eastern policies. They might follow the Western European example and try to keep on reasonably good terms with as many different groups as possible while offering effective help to none of them. They might revive the Soviet policy of encouraging and supporting those elements that are opposed to the West and to Israel. Alternatively, they might conclude that militant Islamic fundamentalism is more of a danger to Russia than to the West. Conceivably, they might discover and develop the cultural affinity that exists between Russia and Israel—a society founded by immigrants from the former czarist Russian empire and recently reinforced by a million immigrants from the former Soviet Union.

The new century has already witnessed the emergence of two new superpowers—India and China. Both possess in ample measure the numbers, the resources and the cohesion for such a role. Both—far more successfully than most of the countries in the Middle East—are facing the challenges of modernity and accomplishing the transition to a new age. Both still have major problems to overcome. These may delay but will not prevent the rise of these two new superpowers to a world role.

Both will inevitably become involved in the Middle East in much the same way and for much the same reasons as the European powers in their day. Bordered by Europe in the west, Russia in the north, China and India in the east, the Middle East will be of vital concern to all of them. Like the great powers of the past, the great powers of the future will meet in the Middle East as allies or rivals, as patrons or masters.

Russia, China and India all have significant Muslim minorities. In the Russian federation, even after the loss of the predominantly Muslim republics, Muslims still amount to some 15 percent of the total population. A significant proportion of these Muslims, notably the Chechens, the Tatars, and the Bashkirs, live in autonomous political entities of their own within the Russian federation.

China, unlike the Soviet Union, has not broken up and retains imperial control over its Central Asian conquests. These include extensive territories predominantly inhabited by Muslims, most of them speaking Turkic languages. The new-found independence of their kinsfolk formerly under Soviet rule has roused new hopes and expectations among China's Muslim subjects; Beijing's policy of setting great numbers of ethnic Chinese in Muslim territories has aroused new resentments. Increasingly, China will have a Muslim problem and a growing area of friction with both the Turkish and Iranian worlds. Russia's experience with the Afghans may perhaps give a foretaste of how this will develop.

India has a vast Muslim minority, much greater than those of either Russia or China. India's Muslims have indeed been described as the second largest Muslim community in the world, after Indonesia, greater than Pakistan or any Middle Eastern country. Indian relations with Islam have been embittered by a long struggle and, more particularly, by the wars with Pakistan. Both India and Pakistan are now nuclear powers, and the subcontinent lives under the constant threat of a major war. As with Russia and

China, but perhaps differently, India will be affected one way or another in its dealings with the Middle East by its own Muslim population. So far, successive Indian governments have been remarkably successful in establishing good and peaceful relations with their Muslim compatriots.

A RETURN TO GREATNESS?

In antiquity, the Middle East was the birthplace of human civilization and of monotheistic religion. In the Middle Ages, it was the home of the first truly international and intercultural society, the source of towering innovations and achievements in almost every field of science and technology, of culture and the arts. It was the base of a succession of great and vast empires. The last of them, in many ways the greatest, was the Ottoman Empire. In the sixteenth and seventeenth centuries, it was a mighty world power— its armies twice reached as far as Vienna, its ships sailed as far as Iceland and Sumatra. Since then there has been no Middle Eastern great power, nor is there likely to be one until the Middle East has resolved the political, economic, cultural and societal problems that prevent it from accomplishing the next stage in the advance of civilization.

The continuing struggle within the region, with the consequent diversion of energy and resources to the politics and weaponry of war, can only make a resumption of outside interference and domination more likely. If the Middle East falls under the rule of China or of a resurgent Russia,

things will be different from the old days. Nationalist dele-
gations will not follow each other to Beijing or Moscow, as
they used to go to London and Paris, to negotiate with their
rulers and put their case before public opinion in the
metropolis. Gandhi succeeded against Britain; the Intifada
worked against Israel. They would have had short shrift
from such rulers as Hitler or Stalin, Mao Tse Tung or
Saddam Hussein.

But there is another way—that of peace and progress.
The second will depend very largely on the first. This
requires from all parties a readiness to compromise on their
own claims and a willingness to tolerate the claims of others. Compromise and tolerance have not been much in evidence in the Middle East in the past, but there have been
intermittent signs of both among some of the key players.
If the different peoples of the region really pool their skills
and resources, they may once again make the Middle East,
as it was in an increasingly remote past, a major center of
human civilization. If they do not, they and their children
face a grim future.

Perhaps the best hope for the region is the gradual if
reluctant emancipation of women. Already in the nineteenth century some Muslim observers noted that one significant reason why their society was falling behind that of
the West was that they were depriving themselves of the
talents and services of half the population—the female half.
Since then there has been some progress in some countries,
but the problem remains a very difficult one, and in large
parts of the Muslim world women are still subject to

constraints and disabilities far worse than anything pre-scribed in Muslim scripture and law or even practiced in early Islamic times. Much will depend, notably, on the development of free and democratic institutions, including the level of participation of the previously excluded half of the population—the female half.

The creation of a free society, as the history of existing democracies makes clear, is no easy matter. The experience of the Turkish republic over the last six decades and of some other Muslim countries more recently has demonstrated two things: first, that it is indeed very difficult to create a democracy in such a society, and, second, that, although difficult, it is not impossible.

The study of Islamic history and of the vast and rich Islamic political literature encourages the belief that it may well be possible to develop democratic institutions—not necessarily according to our Western definition of that much misused term but according to one deriving from their own history and culture and ensuring, in their way, limited government under law, consultation and openness in a civilized and humane society. There is enough in the traditional culture of Islam, on the one hand, and the mod-ern experience of the Muslim peoples, on the other, to pro-vide the basis for an advance toward freedom in the true sense of that word. Even after the toppling of the Saddam Hussein regime in Iraq, the forces of tyranny and terror remain very strong, and the outcome is still far from cer-tain. But as the struggle rages and intensifies, certain things that were previously obscure are becoming clear. The war against terror and the quest for freedom are inextricably linked, and neither can succeed without the other. The struggle is no longer limited to one or two countries, as some Westerners still manage to believe. It has acquired first a regional and then a global dimension, with profound consequences for all of us.

If freedom fails and terror triumphs, the peoples of Islam will be the first and greatest victims. They will not be alone, and many others will suffer with them.

For each and every country and for the region as a whole, there is a range of alternative futures: at one end, cooperation and progress toward peace and freedom, enlightenment and prosperity; at the other, a vicious circle of poverty and ignorance, fear and violence, tyranny and anarchy, hatred and self-pity, leading perhaps in the end to a new alien domination.

CHAPTER TWO

Propaganda
in the Middle East

B EFORE DISCUSSING A SUBJECT as controversial as propaganda, it might be useful to begin with a few definitions and, more specifically, with a few words about propaganda as such. This is a highly sensitive subject, and for many even the word *propaganda* has derogatory implications. But it was not always so. The word, as first used by those who coined the term and devised the procedures that it designated, had a very positive connotation.

ORIGINS

The word *propaganda* first appears as the name of the Roman Catholic congregation or College of Propaganda, founded in 1622 for the propagation of the Christian faith and the care and oversight of Christian missions abroad. This included contacts with Catholic and Uniate Christians in the Middle East. Christian missionary propaganda in the region has continued without interruption from then until the present day. It has been directed principally not toward

Muslims but toward Christians and Jews—to convert Jews to Christianity and to convert Eastern Christians to a Western church. The great struggle between Protestants and Catholics in Europe aroused a new interest in the Eastern Christians who, since they belonged to neither of the warring Western camps, were seen by both as potential allies or even recruits. This new interest expressed itself in study, including the study of Arabic, the main language of the Eastern Christians, and also in propaganda campaigns to gain their support. Enticed by this propaganda, a number of Arab Christians traveled to Europe, where they played an important part in the development of Arabic studies in the universities and the creation of new links between the Western and Eastern churches.

In the meantime, the art of propaganda was itself undergoing major changes. The Thirty Years War (1618–1648) in Germany, between Protestant and Catholic Christians, gave rise to an extensive and increasingly complex political and ideological warfare, in which both sides made the fullest use of the printing press to produce and distribute propaganda material.

The French Revolution of 1789 and the wars that followed brought a new development in the scale and sophistication of propaganda, particularly propaganda for the purposes of war. Until then, war was waged, in the main, by soldiers who were involved by choice. Some were volunteers, responding to the call of kinship or faith; others were professional soldiers serving their government or even—as mercenaries—some foreign government or ruler. In the past, in the West as in the East, forced military service was rare and brief, limited to the time and place of a dire emergency. The Shari'a, for example, defining the military obligation of jihad, makes it a collective duty of the community as a whole, which can be discharged by professionals and volunteers; it becomes a personal duty of every Muslim only when the community is under attack. Universal compulsory military service, as introduced by the French Republic, was something new in military history.

Already in the eighteenth century, the industrial revolution and the resulting mechanization of warfare made the old volunteer and mercenary armies inadequate. The government of revolutionary France, standing alone against all the monarchies of Europe, introduced a new method of recruitment—conscription. A law of December 1793 laid down that "every citizen of France must be a soldier, and every soldier a citizen." A few years later this law was given practical effect when compulsory military service for all became part of the law of the state. Without conscription, Napoleon's wars would not have been possible. Under his rule, conscription was vastly extended, not only to many categories of Frenchmen but also to the men of the conquered and occupied countries.

Enforced enlistment brought, as its inevitable corollaries, obstruction and desertion. In a volunteer and professional army, morale only becomes a problem in exceptional circumstances. In an army consisting largely of conscripts, many of them forced unwillingly into service, morale can become a major problem, and intensive propaganda activity is needed to maintain loyalty. The French Republic and later Napoleon created propaganda of a new kind, designed to bring their message to their soldiers, both French and foreign, to their subjects, and to the peoples of the countries that they invaded and occupied. The combination of revolutionary zeal and compulsory enlistment created a new type of army, which in turn necessitated a new type of propaganda to build and maintain morale.

The French practice of conscription was adopted in a modified form, by Prussia, which imposed a short period of compulsory military training for young men. This practice was followed in time by most other European countries. The English-speaking countries alone remained resolutely opposed to compulsory military service in peacetime and only adopted it, under extreme pressure, during their wars.

In 1798 a French expedition to Egypt, commanded by Napoleon Bonaparte, then still a young general in the service of the French Republic, brought a modern conscript army to the Arab world and, with it, the new style of modern European political propaganda. The lesson of conscription was quickly learnt and applied by both the sultan in Istanbul and the pasha in Cairo. The lesson of propaganda took a little longer.

Revolutionary governments, for obvious reasons, have a particular need of propaganda to justify their activities and indeed their very existence. This point was well understood by Lenin and the Bolsheviks, who made the Russian Revolution of 1917. Combining the functions of agitation and propaganda, they created, probably for the first time since the College of Propaganda, a structured institution officially and effectively dedicated to this purpose. Its function was defined as "Agitprop," and it was concerned not only with politics but also with the propagandist use of literature and the arts, notably the theatre. The Nazi regime in Germany established a whole ministry, officially designated the Reich Ministry of Propaganda, headed by the notorious Dr. Joseph Goebbels, to direct and conduct its vast and ramified propaganda activities.

In modern times, the word *propaganda* has changed its content and has, to a large extent, been discarded by the men of religion, who prefer to denote their activities by the word *mission* or its equivalents in other religions. The term *propaganda* has been virtually restricted to the dissemination of political ideas or the promotion of a political agenda—by the state, the party, the faction, or any other such group. Largely as a result of its use and misuse by authoritarian states with extremist doctrines, specifically by the Soviets and the Nazis, *propaganda* has fallen into disrepute and is now mostly used with a negative, even a dismissive, sense. In most countries and circles nowadays, propaganda is what our opponents put out; what we provide is "information," "guidance," and the like; a form of words sometimes used in modern Muslim states is "department for the guidance of public thoughts." A current American term is "spin"; its practitioner is called a "spin doctor." To describe a statement as propaganda is tantamount to condemning it as a falsehood.

A parallel development may be observed in Arabic. The modern Arabic term is *di'āya*, which has the same negative implications as *propaganda*. Like *propaganda*, it also has a religious origin and derives from the verb *da'ā*. This includes, among its meanings, to call, to summon, to invoke, to appeal, and, in a religious sense, to try and convert another to one's faith. Particularly, but not exclusively, in Shiite circles, the *dā'ī* was the equivalent of the missionary, the *da'wa* of the mission. All these terms have been and are still used with a positive connotation. There are however also negative terms derived from the same root, notably *da'ī*, a braggart or impostor, and the verb *idda'a*, to allege or arrogate or put forward a (normally false) claim. *Di'āya* is a modern neologism and is used only in a negative sense. It is thus the exact equivalent of the present-day use of the term *propaganda*. The positive terms for the same activity are the relatively neutral *akhbār*, information, and the more purposeful *irshād*, guidance.

Propaganda in its Christian religious sense also has an Islamic equivalent in Middle Eastern history. The Isma'ili Fāṭimid caliphs in Cairo attached great importance to the propagation of their doctrines. This task was entrusted to an organization known as the *da'wa*, which maintained a network of emissaries called *dā'ī* , both in the Fāṭimid dominions, to preach to their own subjects and also, beyond their frontiers, to win over the subjects of the Sunni 'Abbasid caliphate. The Cairo caliphs, it should be remembered, were not merely rebellious rulers achieving some kind of local autonomy or independence, as happened in many places during the decline of 'Abbasid power. They were challenging not just the suzerainty but the very legitimacy of the

'Abbasid caliphs. For them, the 'Abbasids were usurpers, and their Islam was corrupted. According to Isma'ili teaching, the Fāṭimid represented the authentic line of heirs of the Prophet, and their Isma'ili doctrine was the true Islam. The tenth and eleventh centuries thus saw a major struggle for the control of the Middle Eastern Islamic world between two competing caliphates, representing two rival versions of the Islamic religion. Occasionally this conflict took military form. More often, it was carried on by means of economic and more especially propaganda warfare.

The propaganda of the Fāṭimids was very elaborate and very well organized. It amounted to a third branch of government, alongside the military and the financial establishments which were customary in Middle Eastern states; a kind of ministry of propaganda and almost, one might say, a kind of church, in the institutional, not the architectural, sense of that term. Its head, the chief Dā'ī, was one of the highest and most influential officers of the Fāṭimid state. In Isma'ili documents, he is often given the title of *Bāb*, Gate, or *Bāb al-Abwāb*, Gate of Gates. We have a very remarkable document—the autobiography of al Mu'ayyid, one of the leaders of the Fāṭimid propaganda in Iran—which describes his adventures there, his journey to Cairo, and his subsequent activities as leader of the Da'wa. When he arrived in Cairo, in about 1045, he found that the mission which he had served, and in which he had placed such high hopes, was in a bad way, and "the product was unsaleable," a remarkable use of modern public relations terminology. The Arabic phrase he uses is *"Al-biḍā 'a bā'ira kāsida."*

"The product is unsaleable" is a fair, if approximate, translation. The Fāṭimid *da'wa* also had an elaborate system of training, hierarchy and financing.

The 'Abbasid caliph and the Sunni *ulema*, confronted with this double challenge, both political and doctrinal, had no choice but to respond. It is in this period that the Islamic institution of higher education, the *madrasa*, was rapidly developed and expanded and assumed the central position that it has retained ever since. In its origin, its immediate task was counter-propaganda—to devise and disseminate an answer to the challenge of Isma'ili doctrines and of Fāṭimid power. As the historical record shows, it was completely successful in both.

TRUTH, FALSEHOOD AND CONTROL

For the present purpose I am using the word *propaganda* in a strictly neutral sense, intending, by the simple use of this term, neither praise nor blame, neither approval nor disapproval. A favorite trick of some propagandists is to convey a point of view by using loaded terms rather than adducing evidence. I shall not use this method.

The primary purpose of propaganda as understood today is to persuade, not necessarily because what one is offering is true or right or good—these considerations are basically irrelevant—but because the propagandist or his employer deems it expedient that the view presented should be

believed and accepted. The propagandist is thus not concerned whether what he preaches is true, nor does it greatly
matter whether he believes it himself. This may have at
most a marginal effect on his skill in promoting certain
ideas. What matters is not whether he believes it but
whether those whom he addresses will believe it. That he
should believe it might be an advantage. It is not—in closed
societies—a necessity.

Some have even argued that the use of falsehood, at least
in wartime, is legitimate. Sir Arthur Ponsonby, in his book
Falsehood in Wartime, published in 1928, puts it this way:
"Falsehood is a recognized and extremely useful weapon in
warfare, and every country uses it quite deliberately to
deceive its own people, to attract neutrals, and to mislead
the enemy." The same author observed, more tersely, that
"when war is declared, truth is the first casualty." The same
point is made in early classical Arabic texts.

FABRICATION

Falsehood is probably as old as speech and certainly much
older than writing. A significant proportion of ancient texts
consists of lies, written with intent to deceive as part of
some propaganda effort. Accusations of falsehood in antiquity are not unusual. Even the first great Greek historian,
Herodotus, acclaimed by some as the "father of history,"
was already in antiquity denounced by others as the "father
of lies." Ancient religion as well as ancient morality show

awareness of the danger. The ninth of the Ten Command-
ments forbids the bearing of "false witness"—the original
text simply says "lies." The inscription of Darius at Persepolis asks God to protect the land from the three great enemies—foe, famine, and falsehood.

In the simpler kind of falsehood, the writer simply tells
lies in his own name. In a more complex and insidious kind
of falsehood, he fabricates written statements and attributes
them to others in order to give them greater credibility and
impact. The same technique may be used without written
texts, simply by starting a rumor. *Flusterpropaganda*, that is,
whisper propaganda, was extensively used by the Third
Reich during the Second World War and then by others. In
the Soviet Union, the manufacture and dissemination of
false news was entrusted to a department of the K.G.B. and
was given a new name—disinformation.

Modern usage has adopted the terms "black propaganda" and "gray propaganda" to designate propaganda
put out under fabricated auspices, the first purporting to
come from the enemy, the second from uninvolved and
therefore presumably impartial outsiders. Though these
terms were of course not used, both black and gray propaganda have a long history.

Even inscriptions can be falsified. A famous example is
the construction text inscribed in the Dome of the Rock in
Jerusalem. As is well known, this great monument was
erected by the Umayyad Caliph 'Abd al-Malik in the year 72
of the *Hijra* corresponding to 691–92 CE. An inscription in
the mosque records the construction, the date, and the

name of the ruler who built it. There is something odd about the inscription. The name of the ruler is given as 'Abd Allah al-Ma'mūn, and the writing is cramped to fit into a space too narrow to hold it. What happened can easily be guessed. At some unknown later date, those responsible for 'Abbasid propaganda were uncomfortable with the idea of such excellent publicity for the dynasty that had been overthrown and superseded by them. The forger therefore set to work to change the inscription and attribute the construction, not to the Umayyad Caliph 'Abd al-Malik, but to the 'Abbasid Caliph 'Abd Allah al-Ma'mūn. The forger did not do a very good job. From the difference in the writing, the name has obviously been changed, and to make matters worse, the forger either forgot, or did not think it necessary, to change the date, so that the original date of construction remains. Most forgers, working in materials rather more malleable than stone, do a better job.

Fabrications are usually of two kinds. In the first, the forger—as in the Dome of the Rock—takes an authentic existing text and changes it to suit his purpose. In the second, he fabricates the text in its entirety and attributes it to a real or imaginary author of his own choosing or invention.

In the early Islamic centuries there could be no better way of promoting a cause, an opinion, or a faction than to cite an appropriate action or utterance of the Prophet—in a word, a *hadith*. The many conflicts of early Islamic history inevitably gave rise to a good deal of propagandist distortion and invention. At a very early date, Muslim scholars became aware of the dangers of spurious or dubious *hadith*, created or adapted to serve some ulterior purpose. They responded to this danger by devising and applying an elaborate science of *hadith* criticism, designed to distinguish the true from the false. Remarkably, the creation of new *hadiths* designed to serve some political purpose has continued even to our own time. A tradition published in the daily newspaper *Al-Nahār* on December 15, 1990, and described as "currently in wide circulation" quotes the Prophet as predicting that "the Greeks and Franks will join with Egypt in the desert against a man named Sadim, and not one of them will return." The allusion clearly is to the build-up of coalition forces leading up to the Gulf War. It has not been possible to find any reference to this tradition earlier than 1990, and it is not difficult to guess when, where and for what purpose this *hadith* was invented.

This obviously spurious *hadith* is a typical example of a favorite technique of the forger. He begins with a "prediction" which is remarkably accurate because it was in fact written *after* the events which it predicts, and, having thus gained the confidence of the listener, he continues with a prediction of events yet to occur. The second, genuine prediction, as in this case, is usually wrong.

Propagandist prediction is not limited to fabricated *hadith*; there have been many other kinds of pseudoprophecies in circulation. Nor is fabrication limited to prediction; many fabrications, devised for propagandist purposes, purport to be historiographic and even documentary. A well-known Middle Eastern example is the so-called Talât Pasha telegrams, a collection of telegrams purporting to have been sent in 1915 by Talât Pasha, then Ottoman minister of the interior, ordering the extermination of the Armenians. The documents were for a long time accepted without question—until their falsity was demonstrated by historical analysis. They have now been abandoned by all serious historians, including Armenian historians, but they are still much used by propagandists. The same may be said of a famous European forgery, *The Protocols of the Elders of Zion*. These were concocted in France in the late nineteenth century on behalf of the Russian secret police; the forgers adapted them from a French propaganda tract against Napoleon III and a minor nineteenth-century novel. The so-called *Protocols* were extensively used in the propaganda campaigns of the Nazis in Germany and of their imitators elsewhere. Though their falsity has been repeatedly demonstrated by historical analysis and even in courts of law, they remain, like the Talât Pasha telegrams, a favorite of propagandists seeking to prove a point and not unduly concerned about the authenticity of their evidence. For a scholar, the question whether a document is genuine or fake is of primary importance; for the propagandist, all that matters is whether he can persuade others to accept it as genuine.

Falsehood, to be effective, must be credible—that is, with the audience to whom it is addressed, even if it may seem comic to others. Thus, for example, the common accusation that all aid workers are really spies may be very credible in a community where no one in his right mind would endure hardship and danger in a far place to help total strangers of another country, nation and religion. For such seemingly irrational behavior, there has to be a rational explanation, and espionage is the most plausible. In isolated individual cases, it may be true. As an explanation of such enterprises as a whole it is grotesquely false—but it can provide excellent propaganda.

Much the same may be said of the conspiracy theories that figure prominently in low-grade propaganda and seem to have a wide appeal. All of us, from the most sophisticated to the most primitive, tend to attribute our own values and motivations to others and to explain their actions and utterances in terms of what we ourselves would do. By this standard, the actions and utterances of others are sometimes totally incomprehensible, and the wildest explanations may therefore acquire a spurious plausibility. Not all conspiracy theories are just theories. There have of course been many plots and conspiracies in the history of the Middle East as of other parts of the world, and these have left their mark on history. But most of the conspiracy theories in circulation at the present time are false to the point of absurdity.

A somewhat comic example is the occasional attempt to attribute a defeat in an international sporting event to some sinister plot involving players, referees, sponsors and, of course, mysterious secret agents rather than considering the possibility that the opposing side might have fielded a better team. Other, more overtly political conspiracy theories, though no less fanciful, are sometimes more sophisticated.

In societies where the legal and social system permits the expression of more than one point of view, propaganda is usually somehow related to truth, and the propagandist proceeds by the selection and interpretation of truth in such a way as to serve his purpose. Total disregard of the truth would be fatal; even the distortion of the truth is hazardous, since, where criticism and contradiction are permitted, any failure in truth is inevitably and immediately seized upon by propagandists for adverse interests. In contrast, in a monolithic political order, of whatever social, cultural, religious or ideological complexion, truth is unnecessary and indeed irrelevant, and, since in general a strict adherence to truth is an impediment to the effective conduct of propaganda, truth in such a society tends to disappear. When the propagandists of open and of closed societies meet on equal terms, the former, schooled in free controversy, usually prevail. For this reason the propagandists of closed societies usually try to avoid such a confrontation. But, helped by coercion and suppression, they can be very effective on their own ground.

Modern technology, however, is making this increasingly difficult. The ban on listening to foreign broadcasts, the control, and in extreme cases the destruction, of satellite dishes and even of television sets may delay but cannot in the long run prevent the spread of the open market in information. Indeed, one of the major reasons for the defeat of the Soviet Union in the Cold War and its subsequent collapse was its failure—indeed its inability—to cope with the information revolution. The maintenance of the communist system and the survival of the Soviet state depended on the strict control of the production, distribution, and exchange of information and ideas. Confronting the challenge of the new information technology, the Soviet leadership faced an agonizing choice. They could reject and refuse the new technology and thereby inevitably fall behind the advancing Western world—just as the empires of the sultans and the shahs fell behind the advancing West when they in their time, for structural or ideological reasons, failed or refused to assimilate the industrial revolution. The other choice was to accept the communications revolution—and thus, inevitably, to lose the total control on which the survival of their system depended.

Other regimes, maintained by the same methods, have faced or are facing the same challenge. A good example is the Islamic revolution of 1979 in Iran. As long as the Ayatollah Khomeini was in Iraq, he was unable to communicate with his followers, even though he was next door. When he moved to Paris, thousands of miles away, he could talk directly to his followers by telephone, thanks to the direct-dial link installed by order of the Shah. He also had at his disposal the resources of modern technology for the production and distribution of cassette tapes. These enabled him to speak directly to vast audiences in a manner and to a degree inconceivable in earlier times.

The Iranian Revolution was the first electronic revolution in modern history. It will not be the last. The regime which that revolution installed has been challenged by the same methods—and those methods have become vastly more sophisticated in the last 30 years, now including fax, e-mail, the Internet, and no doubt more to come.

In modern times, the propagandist thus has at his disposal an immense apparatus—the mass media, radio, television, the press, as well as—in some though not all societies—the educational system. Even in medieval society, before the invention of most of these devices, propaganda was an important element. It has become vastly more so in modern society and pervades almost every aspect of public and, increasingly, even private life.

WHO NEEDS PROPAGANDA?

The services of propagandists, in medieval as in modern times, are required primarily by rulers and those who want to become rulers. Why does a ruler need propaganda? First and most important, he needs it to convince his own subjects of his right to rule and of the rightness of his way of ruling, that is to say, to demonstrate that he is neither a usurper nor a tyrant. It is, of course, primarily those who in fact are usurpers or tyrants or both who need such a demonstration. Legitimate rulers, whether by election or by succession, have little need of propaganda to justify their rule, though they may require it for specific policies. Another task for a ruler's propagandists, again more particularly those of rulers who have seized power by force, is to influence or, where appropriate, to subvert the subjects of other rulers, whether friendly, neutral, or hostile.

Propaganda of one sort or another is always needed by governments at war. This is not limited to a state of shooting war. It applies equally—perhaps even to a greater extent—in time of what we have become accustomed to call "cold war," when countries without formal declaration or the involvement of regular armies make war against each other by propaganda and terror. Terror indeed is, in this sense, a form of propaganda.

Every modern army has a core of professionals; every war brings a surge of enthusiastic, often unskilled volunteers. The professionals are just doing their job. The volunteers respond to the call of blood or faith, and for them their cause is always just, their side is always right, their ultimate victory foreordained. But in many countries, the modern army also includes great numbers of often reluctant conscripts, who are neither following a profession nor inspired by a cause. These need to be persuaded that their fight is good and necessary and—perhaps most important of all—has a reasonable chance of success. This task of persuasion becomes at once more urgent and more difficult at a time when increasing numbers of conscripts are literate, with access to other information and ideas besides those provided by their military superiors. Today, they do not even need to be literate to have access to such other information and ideas. All that is necessary is a portable radio. If it is a short-wave radio, it exposes its owner and his comrades to propaganda from all over the world.

Conscription is very far from democracy; indeed, in some respects it is the very converse of democracy. Yet the two have certain features in common. Both involve the great mass of the population in the processes of government and the structure of power, previously reserved to a small elite;

both, in so doing, empower ordinary people by placing in their hands the means of change—conscription by weapons, democracy by votes. Systems using both tools of governing therefore need to resort to persuasion, that is, to propaganda, to ensure that those weapons or votes are used in the way that they would wish.

At the present day in the Middle East, countries that maintain large conscript armies are heavily engaged in propaganda. Those that rely on professionals and volunteers can afford to take a more relaxed attitude.

Propagandists would also be required by a contender in a civil war or a revolution, in a disputed succession, or any other form of internal strife. Obvious examples are tribal, regional and sectarian rivalries. Propaganda on behalf of employers other than a holder or seeker of power is rare in Middle Eastern history, but it is not unknown, and there are several interesting examples which prefigure modern developments.

SOME THEMES OF PROPAGANDA

The most usual form of propaganda in the past, as one would expect in a region inhabited by Muslims, Christians and Jews, having obvious divergences between and also within these faiths, is religious. The ostensible purpose of the propagandist is to promote the religious beliefs of the side that he represents, to discredit differing, still more opposing, religious sects, beliefs and causes, and to win over their adherents. Very often, this simply means using religious arguments to promote—or oppose—a holder or seeker of power. In the past, Islam, unlike Christendom, had no organized churches or ecclesiastical institutions, and religiously formulated propagandist activities among Muslims tended on the whole to be sporadic and due to personal or sectarian initiatives. This is no longer true. In several Muslim countries, religious hierarchies have emerged, with the functional, though not the doctrinal, equivalents of a church and an episcopate. The most notable example in our own day is the self-styled "Islamic Republic of Iran," headed by a "Supreme Guide."

Another type of propaganda occasionally encountered is that directed against specific tribal, ethnic or other groups, to which the propagandist and his employers are opposed. Already in pre-Islamic Arabia, intertribal feuding found expression in intertribal propaganda contests in which the contenders were the tribal poets, who in a premodern society combined the professions of propagandist, promoter, and public relations expert.

In the first century of the Muslim era, we find a lot of literature reflecting a propaganda conflict between Arabs and non-Arabs, that is to say, between the conquerors and the conquered. At a later date similar propaganda wars arose between other ethnic and racial groups. Religious propaganda similarly could take the form of polemics against the followers of other religions, or, more commonly, against the followers of minority or deviant groups within Islam. At the present time, religious polemics are rare, and where

they occur—as, for example, in the attacks on Judaism—
they are political rather than religious in origin and
purpose.

Unlike many other parts of the world, the central lands
of the Middle East exhibit no significant racial conflicts, and
through centuries of intermarriage the population has
become thoroughly mixed. It is only at the edges—in Sudan
and Mauritania, for example—that visible racial differences
persist. But these have no relevance to the heartlands, where
such differences have virtually disappeared and where the
word *racist* has now become a generalized, meaningless
term, part of a standardized, mostly Westernized vocabulary
of abuse. It may be used to discredit political opponents in
the same way that such other imported terms as *bolshevik*
and *Nazi* have been used in the region to discredit political
opponents. All these terms are equally remote from Middle
Eastern realities, but nonetheless useful for propaganda
purposes.

Verbal Propaganda

Propaganda may be verbal or nonverbal, that is, visual. Verbal propaganda—that is, that conducted in words, may be
written or spoken or some combination of the two. The
recorded history of propaganda begins with the invention
of writing, and indeed, a large proportion of surviving
ancient texts may justly be classified under that heading,
consisting as they do of statements by rulers proclaiming

their greatness, their achievements, their power and often their ambitions or by religious leaders promulgating their doctrines. A major step was the invention of the alphabet and the replacement of the cumbrous writing systems—cuneiform, hieroglyphs and the like—of the most ancient civilizations. With the advent of the alphabet, writing was no longer a specialized craft or mystery, knowledge of which was confined to a small class of priests and scribes. In contrast to the earlier systems of writing, it could easily be taught and mastered, and could bring the message of a written text to a much wider circle. This was still far short of universal literacy, but it was a great improvement on what went before and significantly eased the task of propagandists of every kind.

Written propaganda goes back to remote antiquity and is attested by hard evidence in the most literal sense—writings on stone and metal, proclaiming the name, authority, achievements and claims of the ruler. From early times, these titles and claims were asserted on coins, which passed through many hands; on inscriptions, clear and visible on city gates, in markets and in other public places, as well as on letters and other documents. To these the nineteenth century added two new vehicles—the banknote and the postage stamp. Modern technology has provided a vast new range of means of communication by which the ruler can bring his name, his titles and the claims that these embody to an ever wider public.

The second major advance in the technology of communication, of comparable magnitude with writing, was the invention of printing, which made possible the easy and inexpensive production, on a large scale, of books and pamphlets, newsletters, newspapers and magazines. Printing of a kind was known in China since at least the ninth century; in the mid-eleventh century a Chinese printer introduced a new device—movable type. These were widely used in the Far East, and by the beginning of the fourteenth century had reached Central Asia. During the first half of the fifteenth century these types, previously made of ceramic or wood, were for the first time cast in metal. Between 1440 and 1450 printing from movable, metal types began in Europe. Whether this was copied from the Chinese example or invented independently is disputed among scholars.

There is an interesting contrast in the dissemination of printing and of the paper which it uses. Both were invented in the Far East; both eventually reached Europe, where they enjoyed an enormous development. But the response of the Islamic Middle East to these two inventions was markedly different—a difference that exemplifies the changes that had taken place in Middle Eastern society during the intervening years.

According to the historians, the Arabs first encountered paper in 751 CE, when they won a victory over a Chinese force east of the Jaxartes River and, among other prisoners, captured some Chinese papermakers. These introduced their craft to the Islamic world. By the reign of Hārūn al-Rashīd (786–809), paper is already attested in Iraq, and thereafter first the use and then the manufacture of paper spread rapidly across the Islamic world and ultimately, via Spain, to

Europe. The introduction of paper—a cheap, efficient, readily available writing material—transformed the conduct of government and, more generally, of communication. More relevant to our present theme, it made possible the production and distribution of written material of every kind on a scale undreamt of in the ancient world.

The second great Far Eastern contribution to the technology of writing, the printing press, seems to have bypassed the Middle East. The technology was not entirely unknown. There are some traces of wood-block printing in the Middle East of the Middle Ages and even an unsuccessful attempt in the late thirteenth century by the Mongol rulers of Persia to print paper money. This experiment was not repeated until the first Ottoman government bonds in the mid-eighteenth century. Printing came to the Middle East not from China but from Europe. For a long time it was resisted and was in effect confined to foreigners and to religious minorities. The first printing presses known to have been established in the Islamic Middle East were Jewish and were founded by Jewish refugees from Spain and other Christian countries toward the end of the fifteenth century. The Jews were followed by the Armenians, the Greeks, and the Arabic-speaking Christians in Lebanon, all of whom established printing presses for the production and distribution of books and pamphlets in their own languages and scripts. In authorizing these presses, the Ottoman sultans expressly prohibited Muslims from printing in Arabic characters. The reason usually adduced for the ban on printing in Arabic script is preventing the desecration of the sacred writing of God's holy book in God's holy language and script. Another possible explanation is the resistance of the well-entrenched guilds of scribes and calligraphers. But books in Arabic characters—in Arabic and other languages—were imported from Europe, and finally a Turkish press was authorized and established in Istanbul in 1727. Though it lasted only a few years, it was the first of many. Similarly, in Iran, printing was first introduced and practiced by non-Muslim minorities. Books in Persian were, however, printed in Europe and later in British-controlled India and were imported from both into Iran. The commonly accepted date for the first Persian book printed in Iran is 1817.

NEWSPAPERS

It took some time before the potentialities of this new technology for propaganda were appreciated and utilized. As with so much else in the modernization of the region, this began with the incursion of revolutionary France and the spread of French revolutionary ideas. The first newspapers published in the Middle East were written in French and issued by French government agencies. In the 1790s the printing press which the French had established in their embassy in Istanbul began to produce bulletins, communiqués, and other official French statements. In 1795 the French ambassador began the publication of a regular bulletin, of six to eight octavo pages, distributed to French nationals throughout the Levant. In 1796 the bulletin became a newspaper—the *Gazette Française de Constantinople*, the first newspaper in the history of the Middle East. It ran from four to six pages and appeared at irregular intervals of about a month. In 1798, when the French expedition landed in Egypt, the press was sequestered by the Ottoman authorities. It was later returned, but the French did not resume publication of the *Gazette*.

When General Bonaparte went to Egypt he took with him, in addition to his weapons and equipment of war, two printing presses, one privately owned, the other official. The occupying administration published a French official journal, appearing every five days. They may also have published a short-lived Arabic newspaper, though this is uncertain. What is certain is that the French authorities from time to time issued printed announcements in Arabic, which were posted and circulated. This was a profoundly significant innovation and had a considerable impact.

The first issue of the first real Arabic periodical was published in Egypt by order of Muammad 'Alī Pasha on November 20, 1828. It was for some time the only newspaper, and for long the most important, in Egypt.

In this as in much else, the sultan in Istanbul took up the challenge of the pasha in Cairo. In 1832 the Ottoman government published the first issue of the official *Moniteur Ottoman*, in French. This was followed in the same year by a second journal, in Turkish. Both journals, like their Egyptian predecessor, initially consisted of official announcements, official appointments, judicial reports, and descriptions of the ruler's activities on state occasions. A leading article in an early issue explained that this news-paper was a continuation of the old tradition of the imperial historiographer, an official appointed by the sultan to keep a day-by-day written record of events. The newspaper, it explained, had the same function—to make known the true nature of events and the real meaning of the acts and com-mands of the government so as to prevent misunderstand-ing and to forestall uninformed criticism. This aptly summarizes the purposes and functions of many news-papers in the region to the present day.

The first independent, that is, nongovernmental, news-paper in the region was started by a Frenchman called Charles Tricon in Izmir in 1824. It continued for many years, sometimes changing its name and its ownership. Its open and forthright comments on public affairs sometimes brought hostile reaction from foreign powers. The nineteenth-century Ottoman historian Lûtfi, in volume 3 of his *Tarih,* describes an attempt by the Russian ambassador in Istanbul to per-suade the Ottoman authorities to suppress the paper. He quotes the ambassador as saying, "In France and England journalists can express themselves freely, even against their own kings; so that on several occasions, in former times, wars broke out between France and England because of these jour-nalists. Praise be to God, the Ottoman realms were protected from such things, until a little while ago that man [the founder and editor of the paper] turned up in Izmir and began to publish his paper. It would be well to stop him."

Despite such interventions, the paper continued to appear. At first, nonofficial newspapers were written in foreign languages by foreign journalists for foreign readers. They were followed by publications in Greek, Armenian and Judeo-Spanish, for the religious minority communities. The first nonofficial paper in Turkish was founded in 1840 by an Englishman called William Churchill. After one or two inconclusive efforts, a major Arabic newspaper was started in Istanbul by Ahmad Fāris al-Shidyāq, a Lebanese Christian convert to Islam, in 1860, with strong support from the Ottoman government. This paper, *Al-Jawā'ib*, circulated all over the Arab world and was probably the most influential Arabic newspaper of the nineteenth century. Some other Arabic newspapers were published at the time both abroad, in Marseilles and Paris, and, more important, in Beirut. These were started by missionaries, first Protestant, then Catholic. Both were backed by their missions and churches and engaged in bitter propaganda warfare among themselves. Probably the most influential was the Jesuit-sponsored paper *Al-Bashīr*, published in Beirut from September 1870. The growth of an independent and active Arabic press soon began to cause serious concern to the authorities, who responded in two ways: by imposing restrictions on printing and publication, and by sponsoring counterpropaganda of their own.

The relative freedom of expression brought to Egypt by the British occupation encouraged the emergence of a lively and diverse press, created not only by Egyptians but also by journalists from Syria, Lebanon and other regions. By the present day vast numbers of newspapers and magazines of every kind are published all over the Arab world, as well as in many foreign countries where there are Arabic-speaking populations. Some of these latter circulate widely in Arab countries and have become powerful forces in molding opinion. The first printing press in Iran was established in Tabriz in about 1817; the second fairly soon after in Tehran. Newspapers began to appear from about 1848, first in the capital and then in other cities. The first daily newspaper began in 1898; the first satirical journal in 1900. By the end of the century, newspapers in the Persian language were appearing in Istanbul, England, France, India, Egypt and even the United States.

The newspaper required an entirely new element—the journalist. At his most ambitious, he may appear to combine the functions of the poet, the historian, and the state secretary. Like the poet, and unlike the state secretary, he may—at least in a free society—conduct propaganda against, as well as in favor of, the ruler. The development of the media in the twentieth century enormously increased the scale and scope of his activities and correspondingly increased the opportunities for fabrication and distortion. This aspect of journalism was noted as far back as 1690, by a Moroccan ambassador in Spain. In his report he speaks of the press as a "writing mill" and notes that the newsletters, popular in Europe at the time, were "full of sensational lies."

The profession of journalism, which began in Europe and spread from there to every part of the world, is now firmly ensconced in most of the Middle East and exhibits the whole familiar range of journalist types, form the venal scribbler peddling lies and threats in the service of wealth or power to the fearless fighter for truth and freedom.

TITLES AND CLAIMS

A common form of propaganda in antiquity was through titulature. In earlier times, a ruler's titles were predominantly religious, often embodying a claim to a messianic role. Such for example were titles like al-Hādī and al-Mahdī, the messianic implications of which will be self-evident to anyone with a knowledge of Arabic. Less obvious is al-Manṣūr, literally one given victory by God, with an at least subliminal appeal to the old South Arabian tradition of a Yemenite savior. In the earlier days of the ʿAbbasid and later of the Fāṭimid caliphate, the use of these titles was intended to persuade the subjects that the rulers had come with a messianic duty of establishing the kingdom of heaven on earth. After the first few caliphs of both dynasties, the claim began to wear rather thin, and the later titles adopted by both ʿAbbasid and Fāṭimid caliphs have somewhat less ambitious formulations.

The reference however to prophecies, more specifically messianic prophecies of the kind that were in common circulation, continue to occur. They reappear for example with the Almohads in North Africa, in the twelfth and thirteenth centuries, and some other dynasties that began as revolutionary religious movements whose immediate purpose was to overthrow the existing order and whose follow-up purpose was to establish another order in its place. The titles traditionally used by Muslim rulers, in contrast to those of the Christian world, very rarely said anything about the entities over which sovereignty was claimed. In the traditional titulature of virtually all the monarchs of Christendom, they claim to be sovereign of somewhere and somebody: king of England, emperor of the French and the like. The same is true of the presidents who replaced the kings in all but a few Western countries. Such territorial and national titles were extremely rare in the Muslim world, where rulers used titles that were usually rather vague about whom, what and where the ruler claimed to rule. The primary Islamic title was caliph, *khalīfa,* an Arabic word that combines the meanings of deputy and successor. The office was commonly defined as successor of the Prophet of God, sometimes, more ambitiously, as the Deputy of God, *Khalīfat Allāh.* The latter title was rarely used by rulers and never approved by the religious authorities. The more common title was "Commander of the Faithful," implying authority over all Muslims, whoever and wherever they may be.

In later times, some rulers included ethnic and territorial names in a long string of titles, as for example those of the Mamluk and Ottoman sultans, claiming authority over "the Arabs, the 'Ajam, and the Rum" or over "the two lands and the two seas." They did not, however, in sharp contrast with common European practice now followed by most Middle Eastern rulers, define and delimit their authority in terms

of nation or country. Territorial and ethnic titles were
regarded as demeaning; they were therefore used by rulers
not of themselves but of opponents or rivals whom they
wished to belittle. So, for example, we find a great deal of
interesting propaganda material in the great struggles
between the Ottoman sultans and the Safavid shahs of
Persia from the sixteenth to the eighteenth century. Western
historians writing of these events spoke of these rulers as
the sultan of Turkey and the shah of Iran. They never spoke
of themselves in these terms; they frequently spoke of each
other in these terms. Each for himself and his subjects was
the one universal monarch of Islam; his rival was a petty
local ruler, unjustly disputing his claim, who might be seen
as a rebel or at best as a local subordinate.

During the nineteenth and twentieth centuries, the Middle East came under first the influence then the domination
and then again the influence of the Western world. It was
in particular the target of competing propaganda first from
rival European powers, then from the rival superpowers of
the United States and the Soviet Union. During this period
of intensive European influence, Middle Easterners changed
even their perception of themselves. The most dramatic
example is perhaps the case of Turkey. This name was used
by Europeans as far back as the twelfth century. It was not
used by the Turks themselves until after the proclamation
of the Republic in 1923. Similar changes in nomenclature,
expressing corresponding changes in self-definition, may be
seen in other parts of the region. Thenceforth, Middle Eastern governments, like European governments, claimed

authority over countries and nations and demanded loyalty from countries and nations. These loyalties are known respectively as patriotism and nationalism, both new words in the Middle East; they provide the frame of reference, the language, and most of the themes of modern propaganda both to and in the region. They also define the very nature of identity as self-perceived, sovereignty as exercised or at least claimed, and most forms of propaganda. They normally determine the self-definition of a regime or a country, often laid down explicitly—following another Western practice—in a written constitution. Many of these constitutions, as written, are concerned with programs and principles rather than with rules and realities and therefore belong more to the realm of propaganda than of law.

LITERATURE AND PROPAGANDA

In addition to the obvious vehicles of verbal propaganda, a message can be transmitted through literature, in particular, through two literary forms—poetry and historiography.

In pre-modern times, poetry was in many ways the most interesting and the most elusive of the means of propaganda. In the days before journalists, propagandists and public relations men, poets fulfilled these functions. They were the public relations men of chiefs and of rulers and had been engaged in these tasks for a long time. The Emperor Augustus, for example, had his court poets in Rome, doing public relations work for the empire in general and the emperor in particular. One might even argue that Virgil's great epic, the *Aeneid*, is a public relations job for the Roman imperial idea.

The propagandist function of poetry in pre-Islamic Arabia is familiar to all students of Arabic literature. The traditional classification of the different types of poetry includes at least three that have an important element of propaganda: the *fakhr* or boast, in which the poet makes propaganda on behalf of himself and his tribe; the *madīḥ* or panegyric, in which he promotes his ruler or patron; and the *hijā'* or satire, consisting of negative propaganda against hostile or rival groups or persons. In its earliest and simplest form, as described by the Arab literary historians, the *fakhr* is a technique of battlefield propaganda designed to strengthen the morale of one's own fighters while undermining that of the enemy. A more peaceful form of propaganda was the *mufākhara*, a kind of friendly contest in which poets and orators from different tribes competed against each other, boasting of their own merits and achievements while holding their rivals up to derision. Poets seem at times to have played an active and even important part in some of the wars and conflicts of early Islamic history as propagandists on behalf of one or another individual or faction. There are several episodes in the biography of the Prophet in which different poets appear among both his supporters and his opponents. From the narrative it is clear that their propaganda efforts, on both sides, were considered important.

The Umayyad caliphs, and thereafter virtually all Muslim rulers, had court poets. And not only rulers. There were also lesser figures who employed poets for advertising and public relations. In this way poetry became, for some, a kind of business, and we have quite detailed information about such matters as the rates of remuneration. These obviously depended on the standing of the patron and the skill of the poet and, as in other fields of propaganda, the same material could be re-used. A poem in praise of one ruler could with slight necessary adjustments be resold to another. There are many stories in the literary histories of poets moving from the service of one prince to that of another and sometimes recycling the same poems. The tenth-century ruler of Aleppo Sayf al-Dawla had a considerable staff of poets who, in a sense, are still working for him at the present day, having misled some insufficiently wary historians into accepting the propaganda line. His most famous poet-propagandist was al-Mutanabbī (915–965), a native of Kufa in Iraq, who was regarded as one of the great classic poets of Arabic literature. After having worked for some time as a panegyrist for Sayf al-Dawla, he quarreled with his employer and in the year 957 fled from Syria to Egypt, where he entered the service of Kafur, a Nubian slave who, as guardian of the youthful successor to the rulership, had himself become in effect the supreme ruler of Egypt. For a while the poet wrote great and famous poems lauding the achievements of his new employer. But there too his relations with his master became troubled, and in 960 he left Egypt and went first to Baghdad and then into Iran, where he found new patrons and employers. In the meantime he began to compose ferocious poems denouncing his former employer in Egypt. Kafur was black, a eunuch, and a slave, and al-Mutanabbi made full use of all three in denouncing him.

The Isma'ili Fāṭimid caliphs, as one would expect, had ideological poets. Ibn Hāni', the court poet of the conqueror of Egypt al-Mu'izz, ably presents the Fāṭimid case against the 'Abbasids.

Just as coins and inscriptions could be seen by everyone, so poems could be memorized, recited and often sung, thus reaching a very wide audience.

Some of the chroniclers of the period give us lists of the official poets. Qalqashandī, the great Egyptian encyclopedist of the later Middle Ages, tells us that the Fāṭimids kept a staff of poets attached to the chancery, divided into two groups—Sunni poets who wrote more respectable Sunni praise, and Isma'ili poets who went in for the much more extreme Isma'ili adulation of the ruler as Imam.

Rulers were not the only ones who employed poets for public relations. Poets were also used by rebels and sectarian leaders to disseminate seditious propaganda and sometimes even for purely personal ends. Poetry was also used for what we would nowadays call the social column, as a way of announcing births, deaths, marriages and other events of this kind.

Even at the present day, the poet has by no means lost his importance as a propagandist—to teach, to persuade, to convince, to arouse, to mobilize. Poetry is indeed rather better than prose for the purpose of the propagandist, since of necessity it proceeds not by argument but by emotion and is therefore more difficult to counter or disprove.

The modern poet has several advantages as compared with his predecessors in earlier eras. To spread his message he no longer has to rely on reciters and calligraphers but can mobilize the immense resources of the printing press, radio and television. As in the past, his poems may be set to music and sung—but vocal music, too, in the modern age, is vastly amplified.

What about historiography? That again is an important source of information about propaganda and also, at times, an instrument of propaganda. Sunni historical writing is on the whole very sober. In the Sunni view, what happens is important because it represents the working out of God's purpose for mankind and is therefore a source of information on theology and law, a tangible expression and realization of the Sunna. The Shi'a, by contrast, took the view that after the murder of 'Alī, history had, so to speak, taken a wrong turning; all non-'Alid regimes were illegitimate and all existing societies were, in a sense, living in sin. The defense of the existing order is therefore an important theme of Sunni historiography. Early writing was much affected by this; it was also much affected by the factional struggles of the early Islamic centuries, between family and family, between tribe and tribe, between faction and faction, between region and region. All of these are reflected in the different, sometimes contrasting, narratives that have been meticulously preserved for us by the classical Arab historians.

The historians of medieval Islam, unlike some of their modern colleagues, seem to have been remarkably free from pressure and express themselves with astonishing frankness. They were often ready and able to criticize the rulers under whom they lived, but sometimes they were willing, like historians in other times and places, to interpret events in such ways as to support certain ideas, their own or the predominant ideas of the society. Sometimes, more specifically, they slant what they tell to serve a ruler or patron or, more loosely, a faction, a section or a tribe. There were many such groups, each with its own propagandist historiography.

A major vehicle of propaganda in all societies is the writing and teaching of history. In the past this was done mainly by books. At the present time, pictures of the past may be projected and slanted in many different ways.

Historiography directly sponsored by the ruler, to serve the ruler's purpose, is much less common in the Islamic world than in Christendom. It appears, however, in the time of the Fāṭimids and then more frequently under the Iranian and Turkish dynasties. In the Ottoman Empire it was formalized in the office of the *Vakanüvis*, the imperial historiographer, holder of an office under the sultan whose function was to record the events of the time.

Sometimes historiography acquires an almost epical quality, and here clearly its purpose is to drum up support, usually for a holy war. Two outstanding examples are the Arabic biographies of Saladin and some of the Ottoman narratives of the advance into Europe at the time of Suleyman the Magnificent.

As well as poets and historians, government secretaries could also be employed in the preparation and distribution of propaganda. A form of propaganda much used was the so-called "victory letter," which it was customary for a ruler to send to his colleagues, both friends and enemies, to inform them of some great victory which he had just won. This again has very early origins and probably goes back to the *littera laureata* of imperial Rome and to the Arab *maghāzī*, heroic narratives relating the adventures of the ancient Arabs and then of the Prophet and his companions. Such letters were usually drawn up by some skillful writer and then sent around to other rulers announcing a great and glorious victory to impress them and, of course, also to warn them not to take liberties. A rather splendid example of an Ottoman victory letter records the capture of Kanisza by the Ottomans from the Hapsburgs in October 1600. This was no doubt sent to a number of rulers. A copy of the letter sent by the grand vizier to Queen Elizabeth of England is preserved in the Public Record Office in London. The letter begins by congratulating the Queen on the victory of the English forces against their enemies in Western Europe and then continues to describe, in great detail, the Ottoman campaign in Hungary. The letter ends thus: "Praise be to Almighty God, in this blessed year, both on your side and on ours, such glorious deeds have come to pass. May all our foes be conquered and broken in this way, and may our friends triumph and win victories. In view of your amity to the Splendid Threshold, the Emblem of Felicity from ancient days until this time, and your old affection and friendship to your well-wisher on this side, we have communicated in detail the events of these parts to your noble person. It is hoped that you will keep the door of correspondence and exchange open, inform us of what occurs, and never omit to chastise your enemies in this wise. Written at the end of the month of Rajab 1009 (January 1601) in the city of Belgrade."

The themes and methods of war propaganda have not changed greatly through the centuries—to proclaim and where possible to exaggerate one's victories, to minimize and where possible conceal one's defeats and retreats, and of course to demonstrate the virtue of one's cause and the wickedness of those opposed to it. Modern technology— first printing, then telegraphy, then broadcasting and television and now the communications revolution—has vastly increased the scale and scope of this kind of propaganda. It was war—in the Crimea—that brought the telegraph from Europe to the Middle East, where the first lines were laid by the British and the French in Turkey. The first message, sent in September 1855 from Istanbul to Europe, read, "Allied forces have entered Sebastopol." This telegram was an excellent example of war propaganda—truthful, yet somewhat misleading. The British and French troops had indeed entered the Russian fortress of Sebastopol, after a long and hard-fought siege; but it took a little longer, and more hard fighting, before they captured it.

A uniquely Muslim opportunity for the dissemination of information and ideas was provided by the annual pilgrimage to Mecca. This brought together Muslims from all parts of the world—east and west, north and south—to share in a common ceremony and a common experience. It provided a level of communication and shared awareness without parallel in any other society until modern times. It was also a magnificent opportunity to promote an idea or a cause—an opportunity that was often exploited. In the pilgrimage, as at home, the mosque provided a meeting place where the powers of control of even the most authoritarian governments were limited.

The coming of the telegraph in the Middle East, incidentally, also illustrates another aspect of the impact of the communications revolution. Since antiquity, Middle Eastern rulers have relied heavily on the *Barīd*, or courier service, for the transmission of messages and news and the maintenance of control from the center over the provinces. The Ottoman sultan 'Abd al-Ḥamīd II saw the value of the telegraph to a modernizing and centralizing state and took care to extend it to all the provinces of his empire. What he overlooked was that for every telegraph office there had to be at least one telegraphist with at least enough knowledge of a European language to read the manual of instructions. The telegraphists, most of them young in age and modern in outlook, often found that they had more in common with the Young Turks and other opposition movements than with the government by which they were employed, and the telegraph was an important tool in the hands of those who planned and accomplished the Revolution of 1908.

THE SPOKEN WORD

According to ancient traditions, the two arts which the Arabs most admired and in which they most excelled were poetry and eloquence—the first partly, the second wholly, concerned with persuasion. Classical Arabic literature in general and historiography in particular quote many examples of contests and of victories in which poets and orators exercised their skills in what a modern observer can readily recognize as propaganda.

The advent of Islam introduced a new and immensely important instrument of communication and persuasion— the bidding prayer or, to use its Arabic term, the *Khutba*: the Friday sermon in the Mosque in which the ruler is named. Being named in the *Khutba* is obviously one of the major symbols of authority, going back to very early Islamic times; it is one of the two standard, most widely and generally accepted tokens of sovereignty. Mention in the *Khutba* is the recognized way of accepting and submitting to the sovereignty of a ruler. Omitting the name from the *Khutba* is the recognized way of declaring one's independence of a suzerain in some faraway place.

Already in medieval times the *Khutba* was a major vehicle of communication from the rulers to the ruled. It was an accepted method of proclaiming the deposition or accession of a ruler, the nomination of an heir, and, more generally, the presentation of both the achievements and the intentions of rulers. It was also a way of making known, in suitable terms, such major events as the beginning or the end of a war and, more particularly, the winning of a victory.

In modern times, technology, starting with the loudspeaker and culminating in television and the Internet, has vastly increased the impact of the *Khuṭba*, while at the same time other technical advances, through increased centralization, have correspondingly increased the ability of the state to control it. In some countries the *Khuṭba* is centrally prepared and distributed, and the personnel of the mosques are required only to read it aloud.

But some freedom remains. Even in the most autocratic of regimes, there is one place where meeting and communication cannot be fully controlled, and that is the mosque. That is why the most powerful opposition movements in the region, since the ending of foreign domination, have been religious. The European-style dictatorships and traditional-style autocracies that rule in many countries of the region seek to maintain their power by the strict supervision and regulation of assembly and communication, thus ensuring a monopoly of propaganda. But even the most ruthless and efficient of dictatorships cannot fully control assembly, communication, and therefore propaganda in places of worship. Indeed, by eliminating competing oppositions, regimes have even facilitated the task of their religious opponents.

BROADCASTING

An immense change, comparable in magnitude and impact with the invention of both writing and printing, was the advent of broadcasting and the immense new opportunities which it gave for the dissemination of propaganda by the spoken word.

The invention of radio telegraphy—transmitting written messages by radio over long distances—dates from the end of the nineteenth and the beginning of the twentieth century. The first trans-Atlantic message was sent from England to Canada in December 1901. During the years that followed, radio telegraphy was both developed and expanded. Its use for propaganda purposes dates from the First World War, when the Germans, caught between their Russian enemies in the east and their British and French enemies in the west, used radio extensively to communicate with the outside world. From their powerful radio transmitter at Nauen they also sent communiqués and other news bulletins to the press in neutral countries. These propaganda messages were sometimes effective; but sometimes they were picked up and given prominence by the Allies as objects of ridicule.

Broadcasting in the modern sense did not begin until after the First World War. Its initial development was in the United States, where prescheduled and preannounced news broadcasting began in 1920. This was followed by Britain and France in 1922, Germany in 1923, Russia in 1924 and Italy in 1925.

The first regular transmissions in the Middle East were started in Turkey in 1925, only three years after London. In the Arab states, most of them under foreign rule or influence, broadcasting began later, in Egypt in 1934. In Iran, for different reasons, the national radio broadcasting service, Radio Iran, was not established until April 1940.

But while local stations were still few in number and broadcast only for relatively short periods, the Middle Eastern listener had at his disposal a wide range of mostly propagandist broadcasts, in his own language, from abroad. Broadcast propaganda, on the grand scale, came to the Middle East from the late 1930s and continued through the Second World War and the long Cold War that followed it. During these years, the countries and peoples of the Middle East were the target of an intensive, unremitting barrage of propaganda from rival outside powers—first the Axis versus the Allies, then the Soviets versus the West.

The first foreign country to broadcast in Arabic was fascist Italy, which began a program from Bari, in the southeast of the country, in 1935. Britain followed in January 1938, and Nazi Germany later in the same year. At about the same time Paris began broadcasting in Arabic, and during the war years both the United States and the Soviet Union inaugurated Arabic services. A report in 1966 listed 45 states directing broadcasts in Arabic to Arab countries, 20 in Persian to Iran.

The purpose of these broadcasts from abroad was overwhelmingly propagandist. With the ending of imperial rule and the withdrawal of the former imperial powers from the region, Middle Eastern governments, too, developed their own systems, broadcasting to their own peoples and, on occasion, to those of their neighbors, for information, guidance and, sometimes, subversion.

The first Arab state to organize large scale external broadcasting was Syria, during the period of the Shishakli regime, 1950–54. It was followed by several others. Revolutionary regimes and others established by violence are of course in particular need of propaganda to justify their seizure of power and the overthrow of their predecessors and to protect themselves against the same treatment at the hands of others. And even more traditional, more legitimate regimes find it necessary to resort to propaganda in order to defend themselves against such onslaughts.

The electronic technologies of the twentieth century brought changes at once more profound, more extensive, and more intimate than ever before, reaching, in one form or another, the entirety of the population. This impact is constantly being increased by such technological innovations as the satellite dish, the fax machine, the Internet and e-mail, all of which have vastly expanded the opportunities of the propagandist and at the same time enormously increased the difficulties of those who try to censor or control him. We are approaching a time when even a monolithic political order will no longer be able to control debate and when, in effect, all propagandists will have to compete on equal terms in a global arena. This should give some advantage to the more truthful of the contenders.

In this respect, an interesting contrast is provided by the differing attitudes, during the Second World War, of the Axis and the Western Allies. In Axis countries, it was a criminal offense to listen to Allied broadcasts, liable to the severest punishments, even to death. In Allied countries, there was no objection at all to listening to Axis broadcasts. On the contrary, some British newspapers printed the times and programs of Axis broadcasts in English, alongside those of their own stations. Apart from those whose duty it was to do so, there were few who troubled to listen to English language broadcasts from the Axis. When they did so, it was usually with a mixture of curiosity, amusement and disdain. In a sense, people were even encouraged to listen to enemy broadcasts—the ranting and palpable falsehoods which they put out evoked, among listeners with access to other information, contempt rather than response.

At first, television broadcasting in Arab countries tended to be rather formal and ceremonial, consisting largely of official pronouncements and descriptions. One exception in the region was Israel, which, by broadcasting in Arabic as well as in Hebrew (both are official languages in Israel), was able to reach a certain public in the immediately adjoining countries. As in other open democracies, Israeli television presented many different, often clashing points of view. For Arab viewers this was a revelation, and one at the time remarked what a rare pleasure it was "to see great and famous people banging the table and screaming at each other."

The Arabs were quick to learn the lesson, and the situation was transformed after 1996, when the ruler of Qatar permitted the establishment of Al-Jazira television station. There for the first time Arab viewers could watch, on an Arab station, the exponents of different points of view and different interests, arguing with one another. A second station, Al-'Arabiya, followed.

Since the Second World War the development of television and its introduction to the Middle East has enormously increased the scope of propaganda. Television is not only verbal; it is also visual, and here too it builds on old established traditions in the region.

Visual Propaganda

Islam, like Judaism and unlike Christianity, bans the use of images and makes only limited use of symbols. Because of this tradition, the Middle East has been much less responsive than the countries of Christendom to visual imagery and evocation. Nevertheless, visual propaganda, usually relying on living beings rather than on images and symbols, has often been used to arouse sympathy, to gain support or to project power.

The use of display, of pageantry, of processions, of ceremony, to convey religious and political messages has been familiar in the region since antiquity. It was widely used in the 'Abbasid period and still more in the time of the

Fāṭimids. Some emblems and symbols are primarily religious; others are more specifically related to power, and their use, display and flourishing is intended to strike fear, to overawe or, at the very least, to impress. The spear—the short spear or sword—is used in a variety of contexts, for example by the *Khaṭīb* when he goes up to read the *Khuṭba*. Pictures of birds and beasts of prey, a panther or tiger seizing a deer, a hawk pouncing on some bird such as we can see in the mosaics and frescoes of the Umayyad Palace in Jericho obviously project an image of power, authority and ferocity. The subliminal message is very clear: this is what will happen to you if you do not behave yourself, if you are disloyal to the ruler.

An interesting case of visual propaganda occurred after the battle of Varna in 1444, when a Crusader army sent to fight the Ottomans was defeated and the Ottoman sultan Murad II captured a whole group of Frankish knights, gorgeously attired and caparisoned. He sent them all the way across the Middle East, to Afghanistan and back. The propaganda purpose is obvious: there was the Ottoman sultan, still in an early stage of Ottoman greatness, saying to all his neighbors, colleagues and, of course, rivals "Look at what I did! Look at what I got!" These Frankish knights in full war-kit must have been quite impressive, though they were probably a bit tattered by the time they got to Afghanistan.

The prisoners from Varna were of necessity silent—or at least could not speak in any language which their captors and spectators would understand. Modern technology has added new possibilities, and visual propaganda has become audiovisual. In the twentieth century a victorious ruler does not need to parade his trophies and his captives in person to persuade others of his glory and his greatness. It is sufficient to film them and display the films—in the early twentieth century in cinemas, in the late twentieth century also on television.

Even in the nineteenth century, the invention of photography placed a new and powerful weapon in the hands of the propagandist. Scientists in Britain, France and Germany had been experimenting for some time to find ways of projecting images onto paper by the use of light and chemicals without recourse to drawing or painting. In 1839 they finally succeeded, and thereafter the science and art of photography spread very rapidly all over the world. As with other European innovations, photography in the Middle East was at first in the hands of foreigners, then of members of religious minorities, finally of the majority cultures and their rulers. Armenian photographers in particular played a major role in the development of photography, both as an art and as a business, in the Ottoman lands.

At first it was these two aspects—art and business—that were the main concerns of the producers and consumers of photographic pictures. But other aspects soon developed. The introduction of a postal system toward the midcentury made possible the picture-postcard, bringing images of places and people, and the messages that these could convey, to recipients all over the world.

An even more powerful factor was the newly created newspaper press. Editors soon learnt the value of pictures, with their immediate appeal and direct impact. Pictures, it is said, speak louder than words, and their persuasive power was soon understood and exploited. Such pictures were not limited to photographs in the traditional sense— photographic images of places and of people, from life. Middle Eastern editors soon learnt to adopt another European innovation—the newspaper cartoon, that is, a photographic reproduction of a line drawing. Probably the first cartoon in the region was published in the Turkish newspaper *Istanbul* in 1867; the first cartoon in the Arabic press is probably one published in 1887 in the Egyptian humorous and satirical newspaper *Al-Tankīt wa'l tabkīt* (*Joking and Blaming*). Thereafter, the political cartoon, quickly and cheaply reproduced by photography, became a major instrument of propaganda all over the Middle East.

Meanwhile, interest in the more conventional photograph grew and expanded. Sultan 'Abd al-Ḥamīd II was an avid collector of photographs and built up an enormous collection which was preserved in the Yıldız palace and may now be consulted in the library of the University of Istanbul. Many of these photographs were made to order and were used by the Sultan to demonstrate to the world the progress and modernization of the empire. In 1893 he had them assembled in a set of 58 albums, morocco bound and gold-tooled. Copies of these were sent, with the Sultan's compliments, to the Queen of England, the Emperor of Germany, and the presidents of France and the United States. Their purpose was unashamedly propagandist. Including photographs of industrial developments and military installations, roads and bridges, schools and hospitals, they were intended to show a different face of the Middle East from the familiar portrayals of veiled women, exotically clad men, and strange and picturesque places that had predominated in Western prints and photographs of the Middle East.

Photographs are still extensively used for propaganda purposes, to convey a message, to persuade or to impress. The most convenient and extensive use is in print, in newspapers, magazines, pamphlets, leaflets and handouts of various kinds. Another use is in special exhibitions, arranged for a particular purpose or occasion. Such, for example, are the showcases that some countries display outside their embassies, showing pictures, variously, of their leaders, their peaceful intentions, and their warlike capabilities. Sometimes, after a war, governments arrange an exhibition of photographs of captured weaponry and other trophies, elated soldiers in their own uniform, and downcast prisoners in that of the enemy. Some go further and add stills from enemy newsreels showing burials and funerals of dead soldiers on the other side, with mourners weeping and tearing their hair.

The other great medium of live communication and direct influence through the movement of living persons is of course the theater. In its earliest and most primitive form, the theatrical performance, with costumed performers surrounded by spectators, had a magical purpose: to influence the forces of nature so as to achieve the desired result—usually good weather and good hunting. In classical antiquity, the theater, in a more refined and complex form, had a civic and public role; the message to the audience was often religious and sometimes political.

The three monotheistic religions, Judaism, Christianity and Islam, initially had little use for the theater, with its pagan connotations, and for centuries it disappeared from the Middle East. Some time passed before it reappeared in Europe and achieved new heights in the sixteenth and seventeenth centuries. Shakespeare was certainly no mere propagandist, but his plays, particularly the historical dramas, surely conveyed a message to their contemporary English audiences. The religious dramas staged under church auspices had a more explicitly propagandist purpose, in the original Christian sense of that term.

Theater was reintroduced to the Middle East from Europe in the sixteenth and seventeenth centuries by Jewish and Christian immigrants but had very little impact until the nineteenth century, when it was taken up by modern-minded dramatists who used it as a vehicle to bring their ideas directly to the public. An example was the performance in Istanbul in 1873 of a play called *Vatan yahut Silistre* (*Fatherland or Silistria*) by the Ottoman liberal patriot Namik Kemal. Dealing with a new and explosive subject—patriotism—it was performed before an enthusiastic audience and touched off a crisis which led to the arrest and deportation of the author and several of his associates, under close arrest, to Cyprus. One does not know what the audience made of the play, but its potentially disruptive message was well understood by the authorities. A similar

fate overtook the Egyptian playwright and journalist Ya'qūb
Sanū'a (pen name Abū Naddāra), whose dramatic and literary satires against the Khedive and his advisors forced him
to leave Egypt in 1878. A famous example from Iran was
the one-act comedy *Ja'far Khan Returns from the West* by
Ali Nōrūz. First performed in Tehran in 1922, it dealt satiri-
cally and effectively with the reciprocal ignorance and prejudice with which Iranians and Westerners regarded each
other.

A well established form of theater with a serious religious
message and apparently indigenous inspiration is of course
the Shiite passion play, commemorating the martyrdom of
the Prophet's kin at Karbalā in the year 680. The impact of
this play on Shiite audiences everywhere is immense. But
though it has become traditional in modern times, this passion play is not attested before the eighteenth century and
may itself be due to foreign influence or example.

THE CINEMA

These two powerful media, drama and photography, were
joined together in the cinema, which adds an immensely
important audiovisual dimension to propaganda in the
Middle East. Like poetry, like painting, the film at its best is
an art form, more powerful than either, since it combines
the verbal cogency of the one with the visual vividness of
the other and reaches a far wider public than was ever possible even for the two combined.

The cinema seems to have reached the Middle East at an early date. Silent films, of Italian origin, are reported in Egypt as early as 1897. During the First World War, film shows arranged for British troops aroused some local interest. Local production, at first with foreign technicians and Egyptian actors, began with silent films in 1917. In the years that followed, the Egyptian cinema developed very rapidly and is now among the most important in the world.

The cinema has become one of the most powerful media of communication of our time and as such has not escaped the attention of the propagandist. In many countries, the film, like the book, is restricted by language and is therefore only accessible to outsiders in a diluted form, through translation. But there are some languages—English, Arabic, Spanish—which are used by many nations, and the cinema can provide an important link between these nations and is therefore a prime channel of communication. In free countries, the only message that the film will bring is that sent by those who wrote, made and acted it. In unfree countries, the film may also reflect the instructions of a state agency, interested in its propaganda effects.

The cinema, more especially the newsreel, gives new life and strength to more traditional forms of visual and physical propaganda—ceremonies and rituals on the one hand, parades and marches on the other, including such modern innovations in the region as the ceremonial trampling and burning of the flags of countries seen as enemies. In this ritual one may discern even an element of witchcraft, an attempt to harm the enemy by a kind of sympathetic magic.

A very ancient form of audiovisual propaganda, given new scope by the modern media, is the shouting of slogans or war cries in unison. This was extensively practiced by the New Left of the 1960s and earlier by the Nazi and fascist movements in Europe in the 1930s. Other examples, nearer to us in time and space, could easily be named. The slogan chanted or shouted in unison remains effective as a way of mobilizing support, arousing passion and silencing opposition or even discussion.

PROPAGANDA AND OPPOSITION

It was and is naturally more difficult to conduct propaganda against the authorities than on their behalf. But this was not impossible even in the past, and enough evidence survives to give some idea of how it was conducted. Mostly, propaganda against the authorities was expressed in religious terms. In medieval times its main practitioners were the Kharijites and the radical Shi'a. When possible, they used the same means as the rulers—sermons, speeches, poetry, and occasionally even coins when they had the opportunity to strike them.

During the period of European cultural influence in the nineteenth and early twentieth centuries antiregime propaganda was mostly conducted in political terms. In the Middle East as elsewhere, there have always been ambitious men who seek by violence to overthrow and replace the rulers of their country. These rebels may be impatient heirs, mutinous soldiers, insubordinate governors, or any others whose ambition outweighs their loyalty. Such rebels neither need nor seek popular support and therefore devote little attention to propaganda. On the contrary, they make their preparations in great secrecy, and if they succeed they confront the people with the accomplished fact. They then resort to propaganda to justify what they have done.

Another kind of opposition is based, or seeks to base itself, on a genuine popular movement, and these make extensive use of propaganda. In earlier times such propaganda was invariably religious. Where the state was based on religion, criticism and opposition were necessarily articulated in religious terms. What in modern society is represented by a party and its program in earlier times was expressed in a sect or order and its theology.

In the course of the nineteenth century, a new kind of opposition arose, expressed not in religious but in political terms and proclaiming as its objective not the traditional ideal of justice but the modern ideal of freedom. Most of these movements arose in countries governed by foreign imperialists and were aimed at achieving or recovering sovereign independence. But even countries that never lost their independence, such as Turkey and Iran, were subject to attack from opposition movements within the society. Such were the Young Ottomans in the nineteenth century and the Young Turks in the early twentieth, both proclaiming as their objective constitutional government and freedom under law and producing, both before and after their successes, intensive propaganda addressed to their various audiences—the intellectuals, the military officers, the civil servants and, finally, the people or nation which they claimed and sought to represent.

TERRORISM AND PROPAGANDA

Present-day terrorism is usually propagandist in purpose. Earlier in this century, anti-imperialist terrorism was, in the main, military and, in a sense, strategic. Thus, in the years immediately following the Second World War, three unrelated but contemporary terrorist movements sought by approximately the same methods to achieve the same results. These were the Greek terrorists in Cyprus, the Jewish terrorists in mandatary Palestine, and the Arab terrorists in Aden. All three were aimed, for the most part, against the military personnel and governmental installations of the imperial power in their own countries. All three had as their aim to persuade the imperial power that to stay would cost more lives than the colony was worth. All three succeeded broadly in attaining their objectives. Britain withdrew from Cyprus, abandoned the Palestine Mandate and recognized the independence of Aden. All three decisions were part of the general withdrawal from empire. All three were in significant measure influenced by the cost in blood and treasure that a continuing occupation would have imposed on an increasingly reluctant imperial power.

Later phases of terror in the postwar world were propagandist rather than strategic. The two most obvious examples are the Armenian attacks on Turkish embassy and consular personnel in the 1960s, and the campaign waged by the PLO and more particularly by its more militant components in the 1960s and '70s. More recent examples include terrorist actions against the governments of Algeria and, to a lesser extent, Egypt. The organizers of these actions must surely realize that attacking Turkey or Israel, Algeria or Egypt, is a very different matter from hastening the departure of a weary and already departing imperial power. The choice of target and terrain illustrate this change. In place of military personnel and installations, the new terrorists choose soft targets with much greater publicity value—embassies, markets, schools, tourists, airport lounges. In place of carefully selected military objectives, they choose those most likely to achieve maximum publicity, and instead of limiting their campaigns of terror to their home ground and their enemies, they extend them to the international scene and to uninvolved bystanders. Much of the terrorist activity carried on in the region at the present time has the same propagandist purpose—to impress, to persuade or to frighten.

CONCLUSION

For most of the twentieth century, two ideas, both of European origin, dominated political debate and propaganda in the Middle East—nationalism and socialism. Sometimes the one, sometimes the other, sometimes the two in the devastating combination of national socialism, exercised enormous attraction. Both from time to time enjoyed the active support of European powers. Both were adapted in various ways and with varying success to Middle Eastern conditions and needs. They gained at times passionate support and helped, at least in part, to accomplish major changes.

Today, as the twenty-first century advances, both have lost most of their appeal. Of the two, socialism is the more seriously discredited—on the one hand by the collapse of its superpower patron, the Soviet Union; on the other— perhaps more cogently—by the failure of Middle Eastern and North African regimes professing one or other kind of socialism to lead their people into the promised land. Instead of freedom and prosperity they delivered tyranny and poverty, in increasingly obvious contrast with both the democratic and the traditional worlds.

Nationalism was not discredited but rather superseded by the attainment of its main purpose and the consequences that followed that attainment. With the advent of full national independence, it became increasingly clear that freedom and independence were different things. In some applications of independence, they even appeared to be incompatible.

Nationalist aims have been achieved; socialist hopes have been abandoned. But the two basic problems which they were designed to remedy—deprivation and subjugation— remain and are, if anything, becoming worse. The population explosion has made the poor poorer and more numerous; the communications revolution, with all the opportunities for propaganda that it offers, has made them far more aware of their poverty. The departure of imperial garrisons and proconsuls has removed the excuse for the lack of development, as contrasted not only with the advanced countries of the West but also with other, rapidly advancing non-Western societies. The problems remain and are becoming more serious and more visible. The search for solutions is still in progress; so too is the torrent of accusations and recriminations that obscure and obstruct that search.

In the second half of the twentieth century, the Middle East went through a major transformation, the significance of which has not always been fully appreciated. The first major change was the breakup of the great European empires that had divided and dominated the Middle East and much of the rest of the Islamic world. In the aftermath of the Second World War, the British and French empires were dissolved, and their former territories became independent states. Finally, the last of the great European empires, that acquired by the Russian czars and inherited by the Soviet Union, suffered the same fate. The countries in Transcaucasia and Central Asia that were historically, culturally and religiously part of the Middle East recovered their lost freedom and resumed their independent existence. As in the former British and French possessions, the exercise of their newfound independence has confronted them with a number of problems, both internal and external, in their relations with their neighbors, with each other and with their former imperial masters. There is now a world of independent states speaking closely related Turkic languages and in many ways resembling the Arab world that emerged earlier in this century from the breakup first of the Ottoman, then of the French and British empires. The resulting dilemmas greatly affect the content and form of perceptions, of discussions and therefore of propaganda.

For a while, the end of empire was disguised by the reality of the Cold War, in which, although the non-Soviet regions of the Middle East were independent, their lives and policies were nevertheless profoundly affected by the rivalry of the two superpowers for whom the Middle East was an arena of conflict. This too affected and indeed dominated the whole political discourse of the region, including the content and direction of propaganda.

During the Cold War, the overriding American interest in the Middle East, as elsewhere in the world, was to prevent Soviet penetration and domination. This aim was successfully accomplished, and there can be little doubt that without American involvement, the Middle East would have fallen under Soviet domination and shared the fate, at best, of Poland and Romania but more probably of Uzbekistan and Azerbaijan.

But that is over and finished, and there is no present threat from outside the region. There is of course no guarantee that this will remain so. At some future time the Middle East may again be threatened by a new domination from outside; perhaps by a resurgent Russia, perhaps by a superpower China. Indeed, if the governments and peoples of the Middle East continue in their present inability to solve the problems of the region among themselves, sooner or later neighboring powers may be drawn, even without deliberate purpose, into the politics of the region.

But for the moment this is unlikely. Russia lacks the power, the United States lacks the desire and the European Union lacks both the power and the desire, to perform an imperial role in the Middle East. For the time being, the peoples of the region or, more precisely, the governments that rule them, are free to determine their own fates. For this, they must of course confront their own realities. One can only hope that in making the crucial choices before them they will not be led astray by false propaganda.

CHAPTER THREE

Iran:
Haman or Cyrus?

L ET ME BEGIN with a few generalities about Iran to which I think it is useful to draw attention. In several significant respects, Iran is very different from the region which in modern times we have got into the habit of calling "Middle East." Most of the countries or nations of the Middle East are modern creations, invented by mostly European diplomats and imperialists with frontiers drawn with pencils and rulers on maps. Iran is not in that category: Iran is a genuine nation as that word is used in Europe. It has a millennial identity going back not just hundreds but thousands of years; it is familiar to anyone who reads the Bible and anyone who is acquainted with Greco-Roman history as well as other more recent events in the region. In most of the Middle East—that is to say in what is generally known nowadays as the Arab world—we use the term nationalism to describe the sentiments of loyalty and activism that motivate their political life. The word *patriotism*, which is more common in the Western world, does not really seem appropriate. It is appropriate for Iran.

What we see in Iran is not nationalism Arab style; it is patriotism Western style: a continuing identity through many different changes of culture, of ruler, even of religion and, more important perhaps, a common identity which embraces a great number of ethnic and linguistic minorities, still intensely aware of their common Iranian identity. If you look at the map of Iran, there is one minority after another: various kinds of Turks, some Arabs, Baluchis and so on, all the way round. Yet these are for the most part overwhelmingly Iranian in their sentiments and loyalty, in contrast with other parts of the Middle East, where ethnicity counts far more than nationality and religion counts far more than either. In dealing with Iran, I would say therefore that it is very important not to give the present rulers of Iran the gift of something that they do not at present enjoy, and that is the loyalty of Iranian patriotism.

I will try to clarify what I mean by that as I go along. At the moment I just want to point out that Persian is a quite distinct language; it is not, like the rest of the spoken languages of the Middle East and North Africa, a dialect of Arabic. It includes many Arabic words, just as English includes many French words, but English is not French, and English is not a Latin language. In the same way Iranian retains its distinctive identity even after all the changes that followed the Arab conquest in the seventh century. Persian is an Indo-European language, related more closely to English and French than to Arabic or Turkish, in spite of their geographical propinquity. One can see this by applying the usual basic test—kinship terms and numbers: *mādar* (mother), *pedar* (father), *birāder* (brother), *dukhtar* (daughter), *no* (nine), *deh* (Ten), and so on. It is a language closely related to the adjoining languages of India, more distantly related to most of the languages of Europe. It is also spoken in various forms by a number of peoples outside the frontiers of the present republic of Iran, notably three groups. The first is Tajik, spoken in the former Soviet republic called Tajikistan. Most of the other former Soviet republics of Muslim identity speak languages of the Turkish family: Tajik is not a form of Turkish, however, but a form of Persian, and there is therefore a relationship with Iran that does not exist elsewhere. The second is in Afghanistan, where there are two national languages. One is a purely local one, shared with neighboring areas of Pakistan; the other, called Dari, is a form of Persian, very similar, though with some minor differences, to the language spoken in Iran. The third one—much less important but sometimes in the news is Ossetian, one of those small ethnic groups that are, shall we say, attached to the Republic of Georgia.

Let me turn now to the Islamic aspect of Iranian history and identity. There, as in the other lands that were conquered by the Muslim Arabs in the seventh century, the previous identity was not just lost but obliterated. In all these countries of ancient civilization, as readers may know, the ancient languages were forgotten, the monuments destroyed and even the scripts forgotten. The same is true in Iran. Their history was deliberately defaced. If you go and visit some of the ancient monuments at Persepolis and other places, you can see how the inscriptions and the figures were hacked and destroyed. The writing used in Iran before the Arab conquest was no longer taught or known except among the small and dwindling Zoroastrian remnant, and the Iranian identity expressed in the older culture was forgotten, with this important difference: the Iranians did not adopt the Arabic language as did the ancient peoples of Iraq and Syria and Egypt and North Africa, who all adopted Arabic and became Arabized from the seventh century onwards. The Iranians retained their identity; they retained their language even within Islam; they retained an awareness of being something different. It is true that the Persian language, after the advent of Islam, is written in the Arabic script and contains an enormous vocabulary of Arabic words, often with subtle changes of meaning, but it is not Arabic.

One wonders why it is that the Persians, unlike the others, retained their identity; one can adduce several reasons. One is that people in Iraq and Syria spoke Aramaic, and the transition from Aramaic to Arabic was not all that difficult. But then in Egypt, they spoke Coptic, and there the transition to Arabic would have been more difficult but still took place. Probably the main reason is not language but awareness. Iraq, Syria, Egypt, North Africa, all had been under foreign rule for centuries, in some parts for millennia. They had been conquered a long time before the coming of Islam; they had lost their identities, they had lost their memories, they had become accustomed to being subjects of some external greater power. This was not the case with the Iranians. Their memories of greatness, their memories of independence, indeed of dominance, were far more recent, were in fact immediate, and I think that is probably the main reason why, despite the loss of their history, they retained their identity. They felt the need for history, but since their history was not accessible to them, they invented one. We have the very rich Iranian tradition of, shall we say, "historical mythology," expressed in its best form in epic poetry.

All this is relevant to understanding the place of Islam in Iran and the place of Iran in Islam. With the Islamization of Iran and the adoption of this new Arabized, Islamized version of the Persian language, Iranians, in the early centuries to a much greater extent than later, learned and used the Arabic language—the language of their new imperial masters and of their newly adopted religion—and made a very significant and important contribution to early Islamic culture and history. One even finds occasionally the term *Islām-i 'Ajamī*, "Iranian Islam," so to speak—their version of it as distinct from what one might call the more orthodox (I hesitate before using that word, but it is the best I can think of) version pursued in the Arab countries.

Now one may say, Well, what about Shi'ism; that surely becomes typically Iranian? It does indeed but not until much later. There is, of course, a great divide in Islam between the Sunnis and the Shi'a. Some have likened this division to the difference between Protestants and Catholics in Christianity, a comparison the absurdity of which is easily demonstrated. Just ask which are the Protestants and which are the Catholics. There is no way of answering that

question because it is meaningless. The dispute between
Protestants and Catholics was over ecclesiastical authority;
there is no Vatican in Islam, at least there was not for centuries. In Iran they are trying to construct a sort of pseudo-
Vatican now. That is not the point: Shi'a-Sunni differences
continued for a very long time, but it was at a comparatively
late stage, in the sixteenth century, that Shi'ism became
associated with Iranian identity. That happened when a
Shiite dynasty established itself in Iran and created the
Safavid monarchy, the starting point of the modern history
of Iran.

Now this development was not nationalist. The Safavids
were actually not Persians. They were not even Persian
speakers; they were a Turkish tribe who came from Anatolia
and moved eastwards. If we look at the correspondence
between the Ottoman sultans and the Persian shahs in the
early sixteenth century, the sultan writes to the shah in Persian; the shah writes to the sultan in Turkish. Now, one may
say they are both being courteous, each addressing the other
in his own language. Not at all: the letters in question are
very insulting in tone and nasty in content and prepared
the way for the outbreak of war. The sultan wrote to the
shah in Persian because in sixteenth-century Turkey Persian
was the language used by educated gentlemen, and the shah
wrote to the sultan in Turkish because that was the only
language he knew.

The Safavids from the early sixteenth century onwards
were able to create and maintain (and were followed by
others who did the same thing) a genuine national and

territorial identity. Iran became a nation-state in something resembling the European sense of that term, without any parallel anywhere in the Arab world or for that matter in Turkey. Remember that in Turkey, the name Turkey was only adopted in the twentieth century by the Turks. Previously, the country had been known to its inhabitants by other names: Turkey was what Europeans called it. There is an interesting report from a Turkish ambassador in France in the eighteenth century who wrote a letter full of anger —he had been addressed as "the Turkish ambassador." He found this insulting because in his language as used at that time the "Turks" meant the nomads and peasants of Anatolia. He was the Ottoman ambassador.

It was not until comparatively modern times that identity in terms of nationality and ethnicity came to be generally accepted and understood. In Iran, from the Safavids onwards, it was not Persian or Iranian identity that mattered but the Shi'a monarchy, creating a kingdom sharply differentiated from its neighbors on all sides: to the west, the Ottomans; to the east and northeast, the various Muslim rulers of Central Asia; to the southeast, the various Muslim rulers of India after the Muslim conquest of the subcontinent. All of these were Sunni and most of them were strongly anti-Shi'a, persecuting the Shi'a in their own countries. The Shi'a identity thus became an important part of Iranian self-awareness, particularly in differentiating themselves from their neighbors on all sides.

A word about the names *Persia* and *Iran*: Persia is strictly speaking the name of a province, one part of the country in the southwest, adjoining the Persian Gulf. In Iran, as in many other countries, there were different dialects, and one of them, Persian, came to dominate. Just as Tuscan became Italian and Castilian became Spanish, so Persian, the language of Pars, became the national language of Iran. Those who came from the West and first met that language and first met the people of Pars used the name for the country as a whole, though the Iranians themselves did not do so.

The name *Iran* is closely related to the word *Aryan*— Persian is an Indo-European language related to Sanskrit, on the one hand, and to Latin and Greek and the various languages of Europe, on the other. That also is part of the developing self-awareness. At times it became even a question of foreign policy. In the early years of the Nazi regime in Germany, the Germans made a great effort to win over the support of Iran, and they sent emissaries to tell the Iranians "You are not Semites; you are not of an inferior race; you are Aryans as your name indicates. We recognize you as equals," and so on. And it worked for a while: it did win some good will, not surprisingly after all—it is difficult to reject that sort of approach. Possibly (I cannot say certainly but I would go so far as to say probably), it was at that time that the government of the country began to insist on the use of the name *Iran* instead of the name *Persia*. Previously, the country had been known in all languages but their own as Persia. Now they insisted on the use of "Iran."

This raises the larger question of the pre-Islamic heritage. At the time of the advent of Islam and the Arab conquests, the countries of the Middle East west of Iran—Iraq, Syria, Egypt, North Africa—were Christian and were in due course Islamized, some though not all preserving Christian minorities.

Iran was not Christian. The Iranians had a different faith, an original faith of their own, not brought in from outside: the faith of Zoroaster. Zoroastrians are dualists. That is to say, they believe not in a single almighty God who rules everything, but in two independent supreme powers, one of good and one of evil.

The dualism of Zoroaster is extremely important in human history. The Jewish, Christian and mainstream Muslim God is almighty; the Zoroastrian god is not. He is the supreme power of good but there is also, confronting him, a supreme power of evil, and there is a cosmic struggle going on for all eternity between the two. In some modern Islamic sects and movements as well as in Iran, one can see some relics of Zoroastrian dualism: the belief in a god who is not omnipotent but who, on the contrary, requires the help of humans to fight his enemies and offers them a variety of rewards and inducements to win them over. The struggle continues.

This dualism is very important when we look more closely at the figure of Satan: Satan has a long and complex history. There are two kinds—there is what you might call the Judeo-Christian and partly Islamic Satan, who is either a rebel, a fallen angel or something of the sort, or else a servant of God carrying out some of God's more mysterious purposes—testing for example on God's behalf.

In the Zoroastrian faith, Satan is an independent power, the enemy and opponent of God. This begins to be globally important with the Babylonian captivity. The Jews were sent from the land of Israel to Babylon and they remained there until the country was conquered by the Persians and became part of the Persian empire. We are all familiar with the story of how Cyrus extended his good will, his protection, to the Jews and helped them return to their homeland, and he is one of the very few figures spoken of with, one might say, adulation in the Hebrew Bible: he is described as God's anointed, God's Messiah. The Bible uses terms of praise for Cyrus the Mede stronger than those for any other ruler, Jewish or non-Jewish, and this strongly pro-Iranian attitude in the Jewish tradition continues thereafter.

There were reasons for this continued favor to which we will come back in a moment. One element which may help us to understand the relationship between Cyrus and the Jews is the mutual recognition of a higher religious level. Judaism and Zoroastrianism are in many ways very different but they resemble each other when compared with the polytheistic and idolatrous faiths of most of the ancient world. Their religions were not the same, but they were akin; they could communicate, and they shared the same contempt for the primitive cults that prevailed virtually everywhere else in the region. This mutual recognition and understanding may help us to understand why Cyrus adopted the policies he did toward the Jews and why the Jews responded as they did.

This mutual regard, I think, is generally understood and accepted. What is less generally understood is the importance of the Zoroastrian impact on postexilic Judaism and therefore on Christianity. If you look at the books of the Hebrew Bible and compare the pre-exilic books with the postexilic books, there are certain quite significant differences—differences which can in no small measure be attributed to Zoroastrian influence.

One is of particular relevance, and that is messianism. The idea of a messiah, of an anointed one of a sacred seed who will return and establish the Kingdom of God on the earth does not appear in the older books of the Hebrew Bible. It is a Zoroastrian notion: the idea of a descendent from the sacred seed of Zoroaster who would return at the end of time, defeat the powers of evil in the final battle and establish the triumph of good on earth. This kind of messianism has impact in postexilic Judaism and therefore more powerfully in Christianity.

Let me turn now to the subject of national revival and the revival of national self-awareness in Iran. Here, as elsewhere, the Orientalists played a role of key importance in restoring to the people of Iran some knowledge of their own heritage. The ancient languages of Iran were not entirely forgotten. The Parsees, who follow a form of the ancient religion of Zoroaster, preserved their script and some of their scriptures, but they had minimal impact on their own past and most of them were not in Iran; they were in India. It was the orientalists who first deciphered the ancient writings, the ancient inscriptions and restored to the Iranians, as they did to the Egyptians and the Babylonians and the rest, the knowledge of their own glorious but forgotten past.

I recall a particular manifestation of this change in 1971, when the late Shah decided to have a public international celebration of the 2,500th anniversary of the foundation of the Persian state and, more particularly, from his point of view, the Persian monarchy founded by Cyrus the Great. It was an international celebration to which I had the privilege of being invited, and I was flown there—to Tehran and from there to Shiraz and from there to Persepolis. It was quite a memorable occasion. There was a great statue of Cyrus, and a quite elaborate construction on which all the guests were situated—political leaders, diplomats, academics and others. Then the Shah descended from the sky in a helicopter, landed just by the tomb of Cyrus and made an eloquent speech, of which I vividly remember the last words. He said "O mighty Cyrus, you may sleep in peace for we are awake."

This historical allusion also has an importance, I think, in understanding the role of monarchy in Iran, as a unifying factor. As I said before, there were different ethnicities, different languages, different local cultures, but, along with Shi'ism, the monarchy was the great unifying force, and, for the Shah and his followers, this was a point of which they made very full use.

Another theme in modern Iranian history is that of revolution. As is well known, *revolution* is a word much used in the Middle East: it is the only generally accepted title to legitimacy. All regimes claim to be revolutionary, though most of them have come to power by procedures which would be more appropriately described as coups d'etat or something of the sort. *Coup d'état* in French, *Putsch* in German, *pronunciamiento* in Spanish; the history of the English-speaking peoples happily provides no equivalent. *Revolutionary* is a common, widely used term; every regime claims to be revolutionary. The Iranian Revolution is real. By this I am expressing neither approval nor disapproval; what I am saying is that it is a genuine major transformation, comparable in its way with the French and Russian revolutions, with parallel themes and parallel phases, and it now appears to be entering what one might describe as either the Stalin or the Napoleon phase. The Iranians would probably prefer to call it the Napoleon phase; I think it would be more accurate to call it the Stalin phase. The initial Western reaction to the Iranian Revolution was a very positive one, particularly in the United States where it is generally believed that any movement to establish a republic in place of a monarchy must be progressive and therefore good.

There was considerable reluctance to recognize the reality of what was happening in Iran. At the time of the Iranian Revolution I was in Princeton. I had been in Iran not long previously, but when it happened I was back home, reading the newspapers and listening to the news. There was a great deal of talk about this man Khomeini. I must confess I had never heard the name Khomeini before, but I did what we normally do in our profession: I went to the university library and looked him up in the catalogue to see if there was anything either by him or about him. And I found a little book called *Islamic Government* written by the said Khomeini. It was available in both Persian and Arabic, but not, at that time, in any Western language. I checked the book out and read it and this made it very clear who he was and what his aims were; and the popular idea that this was going to mean the establishment of a liberal, open, modern society in place of the reactionary Shah was utter nonsense.

The problem was how to make this disagreeable fact known. It took a long time before it was possible to persuade either the media or officialdom of the existence of this book, of its contents and its meaning, and of who Khomeini was and what he was going to do.

I think by now we have all lost whatever illusions we may have had about the regime, though some people have substituted a different set of illusions.

By now the Iranian Revolution is seen as a major threat in the region, and it is in the sense that it is reaching out— eastward to Afghanistan and Pakistan, westward to Iraq, where it has been playing a major role in the various disorders that have plagued that country, and beyond Iraq by the northern route to Syria and to Lebanon and by the southern route to Hamas in Gaza. The fact that one is Sunni and the other is Shi'a does not seem to bother them. The common enemy overrides what have become relatively minor differences among themselves.

Because of this expansion, there is a growing concern in the Muslim Middle East, particularly in the strongly Sunni countries such as Egypt and Saudi Arabia, who see this as a real danger, and it is a real danger for two reasons. One is the Shi'a reason: there are significant Shi'a minorities in Kuwait, in Saudi Arabia and in the other Gulf states—even some Shi'a majorities, locally at least—who have been suppressed and disenfranchised in most ways. The Iranian Revolution has awakened them, and they are seen, with some justification, as a major threat to the existing regimes. It was perfectly clear, in the war that Israel fought against Hezbollah in 2006, that the Sunni Arab states were quietly hoping the Israelis would do the job and finish it and were manifestly disappointed when the Israelis failed to do so. This growing concern has interesting parallels with Sadat's fears of Soviet domination. It was the fear of Soviet domination rather than any goodwill to Israel which led him to seek peace against what he saw rightly as the more dangerous enemy, and clearly there are a number now in the Arab world, including near neighbors, who take the same view. If we look at the reactions to what has been happening in Gaza, one cannot but be struck by the relative silence on the West Bank, for example, and elsewhere. This creates, I think, a new and interesting situation.

In looking at the Iranian Revolution, we must also be concerned by what I would call the apocalyptic aspect of it, the fact that these people really believe that this is the final stage. Most religions, certainly Judaism, Christianity and

Islam, share a belief in an end-of-time scenario when God's anointed (however he may be defined) will come and fight God's enemy in the final battle and establish the Kingdom of God on earth, when all the wicked will go to eternal damnation and the good will enjoy the eternal delights of paradise, as variously described.

Awareness of the threat of mutual assured destruction, was an effective deterrent during the Cold War in both the United States and the Soviet Union. Both had nuclear weapons as also did some other powers. But they did not use them because they knew that if they did use them, the others would respond in kind, and the fear of mutual assured destruction was a way of keeping the peace. This does not quite work at the present time because of the apocalyptic view. With these people's apocalyptic mindset, mutual assured destruction is not a deterrent, it is an inducement; it is a quick free pass for the true believers to heaven and its delights and the dispatch of the rest to hell.

This raises the interesting and relevant question of the Devil. In Iran, the common practice is to speak of the United States and Israel as the Great Satan and the Little Satan. Generally speaking, there is a not very sharp but nevertheless discernible difference of opinion between those who hate America because America is Israel's patron and those who hate Israel because Israel is America's protégé. They overlap but they are distinct and the different themes can be seen in various groups and writings. For the Iranian leadership, the United States is the major adversary, the leader of the world of the infidels in succession to the long series of leaders who ruled the world of infidels. Against them, the Iranians now see themselves as the rulers of the world of true Islam. This coincides to a quite remarkable extent with the al-Qaeda perception of the struggle—again, the United States as the global infidel satanic force. What I find interesting is that in some Iranian writings about the role of the United States as the satanic force, the word they use is not *Shaitan*, which is the Islamic equivalent of Satan, but *Ahriman*, which is the Zoroastrian term for the supreme figure of evil. More recently, in the demonstrations after the Iranian election in June 2009, the crowds denounced the president, calling him "Ahriman-nejad."

Let me turn now to another aspect: the resulting attitudes toward Jews and Israel. Here I think the two names that I put in the title—Haman and Cyrus—may serve to typify two long-standing traditions. The treatment of Cyrus by the Jewish historiographic tradition is quite remarkable: he appears as a messianic figure, and during the periods of Persian rule, there were no complaints, no rebellions. There were problems now and then, problems with the *Resh-Galuta*, the officially recognized head of the Jewish community, who got into trouble with the authorities, but these were generally speaking seen as very minor problems and did not affect the genuine relationship. Cyrus, as I remarked before, is presented even in the Bible as God's anointed, and the period of Persian rule in Babylonia is still seen as a golden age in Jewish history, especially the early centuries of the Common Era, before the advent of Islam—when Syria, Palestine and Egypt were ruled by the Byzantine empire and when Babylonia (Iraq) was ruled by the Persians and the Jews were headed by their own chief, the *Resh-Galuta*. Jews were accused by the Byzantines of being a Persian fifth column; they were suspected (and there is some evidence that these suspicions were not without foundation) of being pro-Persian and anti-Byzantine. The clearest evidence of this is in the early seventh century, when the Persians invaded Palestine and captured Jerusalem, where they were welcomed enthusiastically by the Jewish population and stayed for a number of years, after which the Byzantines were able to recover the city, drive out the Persians and then carry out a major massacre of the Jews.

What about Haman? According to the widely held opinion, the Haman-Esther story as contained in the Bible is probably mythic. We are indeed told in the Talmud that the Book of Esther was not originally included in the Hebrew Bible, but it was finally included because of its popularity among the people. It was not part of the original choice. If you look at the book, it is in many ways suspicious, starting with the names—Esther and Mordechai. One thinks of the Babylonian Ishtar and Marduk, a rather remarkable resemblance. Nevertheless the Haman-Esther story does, I think, give us a first account of the other Iranian tradition, the tradition of hostility. It is expressed through the personality (be it historic or mythic) of the Persian dignitary Haman, whose main purpose in life seems to be to make life difficult, if not impossible, for Jews. This hostility continues, though not in the pre-Islamic period; at least it is not documented. There are occasional difficulties but nothing of any consequence, nothing that is retained, shall we say, by the Jewish historiographic tradition.

But with the advent of Islam and the adoption of Shi'ism, it is quite a different story. Iranian Islam is much more intolerant of Jews than in most other versions of Islam. There was, for example, the idea that the Jews were *nijis*— unclean—that anything touched by a Jew became unclean and could not be used or eaten. There was a whole elaborate development of this doctrine of what one might call "untouchability" since it is obviously related to the kindred Aryan doctrine of untouchability in the neighboring country of India.

This attitude continued, and if we look at the position of the Jews in well-documented semimodern periods it is clear that the Jews were very badly treated; they were treated, as I said, as untouchables and subjected to all kinds of indignities and humiliations. It is in the same tradition that, in the language of the Islamic Republic today, Jews are usually depicted as vermin or something of the sort. "Cancerous microbes" is the phrase that is often used.

There is some difference between the external and internal language used in Iran at the present day; for example in slogans draped over military vehicles, the English text says "Down with . . ." and the Persian text says "Marg bar," which means "Death to. . . ." Death to is not exactly the same as "down with," though I doubt if there would be much difference if the Iranians were able to realize their purpose.

Let me end with some quotations; one from Khomeini: "A billion Muslims should unite and defeat America." This was basically the purpose of the Iranian Revolution; this was what it was all about for him and his followers— confronting the ultimate enemy, the Great Satan, compared with which Little Satan was of relatively minor importance. Here is another quotation from Khomeini: "The Americans will run away [from the Middle East] leaving their illegitimate child [Israel] behind them, and then the Muslims will know what to do." Ahmadinejad many times, when addressing the Arabs, uses this formula and also has made the point that the Middle East has become the battleground between the Muslims and the infidel West. In other words, it is not the Middle East as such that matters; it is now the battleground between the two great global forces—the force of good and the force of evil.

What are the possibilities in dealing with this threat from Iran? I think one can divide them into two: one is the obvious military one. It may reach a point when there is no other; I do not personally believe that we have reached that point yet, and I believe that, even in talking about it, it is very important not to give the regime a free gift of something that they do not at present enjoy, that is, the support of Iranian patriotism. This needs careful handling: for example, if one says, "Iran must not have nuclear weapons," the answer is that we all agree on that. But try to look at it from the point of view of an Iranian patriot, not a supporter of the regime necessarily. He would say, "To the north there is a nuclear-armed Russia; to the east a nuclear-armed China; to the south a nuclear-armed India and Pakistan; to the west a nuclear-armed Israel. Who is to say that we must not have it?" It is obvious why they must not have it: none of the others are proposing to obliterate anybody. But I am trying to put the question as it might appear to an otherwise well-disposed Iranian patriot. I think one has to handle this very carefully and before deciding that the military option is the only one that remains. There are possibilities internally within Iran, opportunities which I think have been underused or totally neglected. One thinks, for example, of the bus strike not long ago—a quite remarkable opportunity, but nothing was done about it. It seems to me that, for the moment, one should aim at disruption rather than a military action, but I must, in concluding, admit the possibility that one may, at some time, reach a situation when there is no other option available.

CHAPTER FOUR

The New Anti-Semitism—
First Religion,
Then Race,
Then What?

T HERE IS A WELL-WORN PLATITUDE that we have all heard many times before: it is perfectly legitimate to criticize the actions and policies of the state of Israel or the doctrines of Zionism without necessarily being motivated by anti-Semitism. The fact that this has been repeated ad nauseam does not detract from its truth. Not only do I accept it, but I would even take it a step further with another formulation that may perhaps evoke surprise if not shock: it is perfectly possible to hate and even to persecute Jews without necessarily being anti-Semitic.

Unfortunately, hatred and persecution are a normal part of the human experience. Taking a dislike, mild or intense, to people who are different in one way or another, by ethnicity, race, color, creed, eating habits—no matter what—is part of the normal human condition. We find it throughout recorded history, and we find it all over the world. It can sometimes be extraordinarily vicious and sometimes even amusing.

Not long after the Second World War, the Danes were seething with resentment against two of their neighbors: the Germans, for having occupied them, and the Swedes, for having stood by with unhelpful neutrality. A Danish saying current at the time was: What is a Swede? A German in human form. Another double-barreled insult, this one from the British army in the late 1930s, when it was concerned about two different groups of terrorists: What is an Arab? A toasted Irishman. I quote these not in any sense with approval or commendation but as examples of the kind of really nasty prejudice that is widespread in our world.

Anti-Semitism is something quite different. It is marked by two special features. One of them is that Jews are judged by a standard different from that applied to others. We see plenty of examples of this at the present time, but here, too, one has to be careful. There can be different standards of judgment on other issues too, sometimes even involving Jews, that are not necessarily motivated by anti-Semitism.

For instance, in mid-September 1975 in Spain, five terrorists convicted of murdering policemen were sentenced to death. European liberal opinion was outraged that in this modern age a Western European country should sentence people to death. Unheard of!—there was an outcry of indignation, and strong pressures were brought to bear on the Spanish government. But in the Soviet Union and its satellite states during the same period, vastly greater numbers were being sentenced to death and executed; and, in Africa, Idi Amin was slaughtering hundreds of thousands, a large part of the population of Uganda. There was hardly a murmur of protest in the Western world.

The lesson is very clear. Right-wing governments (General Francisco Franco was still in charge in Spain) are not allowed to sentence offenders to death; left-wing governments are. There is a further implication: slaughter of or by white people is bad; slaughter of or by people of color is normal. Similar discrepancies may be found in responses to a number of other issues, as for example the treatment of women and of ethnic or other minorities.

These examples show that even a wide disparity of standards of judgment is not necessarily in itself evidence of anti-Semitism. There may be other elements involved. For example, the comparison is sometimes made between the world reaction to the massacre of Palestinians by Lebanese Christian militiamen at Sabra and Shatila in September 1982, where some 800 people were killed, and the massacre earlier in the same year in Hama in Syria, where tens of thousands were killed. On the latter, not a dog barked. The difference, of course, was in the circumstances. In both cases the perpetrators were Arab, but in the case of Sabra and Shatila, because of the dominant Israeli military presence in the region, there was a possibility of blaming the Jews. In Hama, this possibility did not exist; therefore the mass slaughter of Arabs by Arabs went unremarked, unnoticed and unprotested. This contrast is clearly anti-Jewish. In a different way, it is also anti-Arab.

We see other instances of differing standards and methods of judgment nearer home and in a perhaps less alarming form. We hear a great deal, for example, about the

Jewish lobby and the various accusations that are from time to time brought against it, that those engaged in it are somehow disloyal to the United States and are in the service of a foreign power.

The Jewish lobby is, of course, not the only lobby of its kind. Consider three others: the Irish, Greek, and Armenian lobbies. The Irish lobby, which campaigned against the United Kingdom, America's closest ally, and the Greek and Armenian lobbies, which campaigned against Turkey when Turkey was a crucial NATO ally, were seen as pursuing their legitimate concerns. I do not recall accusations against any of them of disloyalty or even of divided loyalty.

The other special feature of anti-Semitism, which is much more important than differing standards of judgment, is the accusation against Jews of cosmic evil. Complaints against people of other groups rarely include it. This accusation of cosmic, satanic evil attributed to Jews, in various parts of the world and in various forms, is what has come to be known in modern times as anti-Semitism.

In the Western world, anti-Semitism has gone through three clearly distinct phases. Some people have written and spoken about anti-Semitism in antiquity, but the term in that context is misleading. We do indeed find texts in the ancient world attacking and denouncing Jews, sometimes quite viciously, but we also find nasty remarks about Syrians, Egyptians, Greeks, Persians and the rest. There is no great difference between the anti-Jewish remarks and the ethnic and religious prejudices expressed against other peoples, and on the whole the ones against Jews are not the most vicious. The Syrian-born Roman historian Ammianus Marcellinus, for example, speaking of the Saracens, remarks that they are not to be desired either as friends or as enemies. I do not recall, in the ancient world, anything said about the Jews quite as nasty as that.

Polytheism was essentially tolerant, each group worshiping its own god or gods, offering no objection to the worship of others. Indeed, one might have been willing to offer at least a pinch of incense to some alien god in courtesy as a visitor or, even at home, in deference to a suzerain. Only the Jews in the ancient world insisted—absurdly, according to the prevailing view of the time—that theirs was the only god and that the others did not exist. This gave rise to problems with their neighbors and their various imperial masters, notably the Romans. It sometimes provoked hostile comments and even persecution but not the kind of demonization that has come to be known as anti-Semitism. The tendency was rather to ridicule the Jews for their faceless, formless god in the clouds and for such absurd and barbarous customs as circumcision, the rejection of pig meat and, most absurd of all, the Sabbath. Several Greek and Roman authors noted that because of this comic practice the Jews were wasting one-seventh of their lives.

Demonization, as distinct from common or garden-variety prejudice or hostility, began with the advent of Christianity and the special role assigned to the Jews in the crucifixion of Christ as related in the Gospels. Christianity started as a movement within Judaism, and the conflict between Christians and Jews had that special bitterness that often makes conflicts within religions more deadly than those between religions. The Christian message was presented as the fulfillment of God's promises to the Jews, written in what Christians called the Old Testament. The rejection of that message by the Jewish custodians of the Old Testament was especially wounding.

An important concern of the early Christians was not so much to blame the Jews as, for understandable reasons, to exculpate the Romans. Jewish guilt and Roman innocence, the two interdependent, became important parts of the Christian message, first to Rome and then beyond, with devastating effect on popular attitudes toward Jews, especially at Easter time.

For many centuries, hatred and persecution of Jews, and the ideology and terminology used to express them, were grounded in religion. Then came the phase when religious prejudice was discredited, seen as not in accord with the ideas of the Enlightenment. It was seen as bigoted; worse, as old-fashioned, out-of-date. That meant new reasons were needed for hating Jews. They were found.

The process of change began in Spain when large numbers of Jews—and also Muslims—were forcibly converted to Christianity. With a forcible conversion there was inevitably some doubt, especially among the enforcers, as to the sincerity of the converts. And this doubt was well grounded, as we know from the phenomenon of the Marranos and the Moriscos, the sometimes dubious converts from Judaism and Islam. Thus, the practice arose of examining the racial origins of the so-called new Christians. We even find statutes in sixteenth-century Spain about purity of blood, *la limpieza de sangre*. Only people who could prove Christian descent for a specified number of generations could be accepted as genuine Christians. "Purity of blood" was required for certain positions and certain offices.

This is where the racial form of anti-Semitism began. It was systematized in Germany in the nineteenth century, when for the first time the term *anti-Semitism* was invented and adopted.

Semitic was first used as a linguistic, not an ethnic or racial, term. Like *Aryan*, it was coined by philologists to designate a group of related languages. Aryan included languages as diverse as Sanskrit, Persian and, by extension, Greek, Latin and most of the languages of Europe. Semitic, similarly, brought together Syriac, Arabic, Hebrew, and Ethiopic. Already in 1872 the great German philologist Max Miller pointed out that *Aryan* and *Semitic* were philological, not ethnological, terms and that to speak of an Aryan or Semitic race was as absurd as to speak of a dolichocephalic (longheaded) language. "What misunderstandings, what controversies would arise," he said, from confusing the two—a correct if understated prediction.

Despite these warnings, *Semitic* was transferred from its original linguistic meaning to a new racial meaning and became the basis for a new and different bigotry. The people who advocated this bigotry spurned religious prejudice because they saw themselves as modern and scientific. Their hostility to Jews, they claimed, was based on observed and documented racial otherness and inferiority.

And then, just as religious hostility was spurned by the Enlightenment and replaced by modern and "scientific" racial hostility, so racial hostility was discredited by the Third Reich and its crimes, by the revelations after its fall of the appalling things that it had done. This discrediting of racism left a vacancy, an aching void.

This is where the third phase of anti-Semitism arises, which for want of a better term we might call political-cum-ideological Judeophobia. Race? Oh no, we wouldn't have anything to do with that. Religious prejudice? Oh no, we're far beyond that. This is political and ideological, and it provides a socially and intellectually acceptable modern disguise for sentiments that go back some two thousand years.

Turning from the Christian to the Islamic world, we find a very different history. If we look at the considerable literature available about the position of Jews in the Islamic world, we find two well-established myths. One is the story of a golden age of equality, of mutual respect and cooperation, especially but not exclusively in Moorish Spain; the other is of subservience and persecution and ill treatment. Both are myths. Like many myths, both contain significant elements of truth, and the historic truth is in its usual place, somewhere in the middle between the extremes.

There are certain important differences between the treatment, the position, and the perception of Jews in the premodern Islamic world and in the premodern and also modern Christian worlds.

The story of a golden age of complete equality is, of course, nonsense. No such thing was possible or even conceivable. Indeed, among Christians and Muslims alike, giving equal rights or, more precisely, equal opportunities to unbelievers would have been seen not as a merit but as a dereliction of duty. But until fairly modern times there was a much higher degree of tolerance in most of the Islamic lands than prevailed in the Christian world. For centuries, in most of Europe, Christians were very busy persecuting each other; in their spare time, they were persecuting Jews and expelling Muslims—all at a time when, in the Ottoman Empire and some other Islamic states, Jews and several varieties of Christians were living side by side fairly freely and comfortably.

The comparison has often been made between the Cold War of the twentieth century and the confrontation between Christendom and Islam in the fifteenth, sixteenth, and seventeenth centuries. In many ways the comparison is a good one. But one has to remember that in the confrontation between Christendom and Islam, the movement of refugees, of those who, in Lenin's famous phrase, "voted with their feet," was overwhelmingly from west to east not from east to west.

The reason for this was tolerance and no more than that. Tolerance is by modern standards an essentially intolerant idea. Tolerance means that I am in charge. I will allow you some though not all of the rights and privileges that I enjoy, provided that you behave yourself according to rules that I will lay down and enforce. That seems a fair definition of tolerance as usually understood and applied. By modern standards, it is an intolerant idea, but it is a lot better than intolerance as such, and the limited but substantial tolerance accorded to Jews and other non-Muslim communities in the Muslim states until early modern times was certainly vastly better than anything that was available in Christendom.

Prejudices existed in the Islamic world, as did occasional hostility, but not what could be called anti-Semitism, for there was no attribution of cosmic evil. And on the whole, Jews fared better under Muslim rule than Christians did. This is the reverse of what one might expect. In the canonical history, in the Qur'ān and the biography of the Prophet, Jews come out badly. The Prophet had more encounters with Jews than with Christians, so we find more negative statements about Jews than about Christians. The biography of the Prophet records armed clashes with Jews, and in those encounters it was the Jews who were killed. Muslims could therefore afford a more relaxed attitude toward Jews in the ensuing generations.

The other advantage for Jews was that they were not seen as dangerous. Christianity was recognized as a rival world religion and a competitor in the cosmic struggle to bring enlightenment (and with it, inevitably, domination) to all humanity. This cosmic competition had important consequences. Local Christians were dangerous in that they were a potential fifth column for the Christian powers of Europe, the main adversary of the Islamic world. Jews were not suspected of being pro-Christian. On the contrary, they were seen as being reliable and even useful. It was not merely tolerance or goodwill—though these were essential preconditions—that led the Ottoman sultans to admit so many

Jewish refugees from Spain, Portugal, Italy and elsewhere. Jews, especially those of European origin, were active in trade and industry, and, from many documents in the Ottoman archives, it is clear that they were valued as a revenue-producing asset. They were not just permitted; they were encouraged and even on a few occasions compelled to settle in Ottoman lands, especially in newly conquered provinces.

Obviously, this is not equality, but it is not anti-Semitism in any sense of the word either. The Ottomans' treatment of the Jews even included a kind of respect. We do of course find expressions of prejudice against the Jews, as against any group of people that are different, but their general attitude was of amused, tolerant superiority.

An interesting difference in hostile stereotypes can be found in anecdotes, jokes and the like. The main negative quality attributed to Jews in Turkish and Arab folklore was that they were cowardly and unmilitary—very contemptible qualities in a martial society. A late Ottoman joke may serve to illustrate this. The story is that in 1912, at the time of the Balkan war, when there was an acute threat to the Ottoman Empire in its final stages, the Jews, full of patriotic ardor, decided that they, too, wanted to serve in the defense of their country, so they asked permission to form a special volunteer brigade. Permission was given, and officers and noncommissioned officers were sent to train and equip them. Once the Jewish volunteer brigade was armed, equipped and trained, ready to leave for the front, they sent a message asking if they could have a police escort because there were reports of bandits on the road.

This is a very interesting human document. Is it hostile? Not really. It shows a sort of amused tolerance, at once good humored and contemptuous, that may help us to understand the bewilderment and horror at the Israeli victories in 1948 and after. We have some vivid descriptions at the time of the expectations and reactions of 1948. Abdul Rahman Azzam Pasha, who was then the secretary-general of the Arab League, is quoted as having said: "This will be like the Mongol invasions. We will utterly destroy them. We will sweep them into the sea." The expectation was that it would be quick and easy. There would be no problem at all dealing with half a million Jews. It was then an appalling shock when five Arab armies were defeated by half a million Jews with very limited weaponry. It remains shameful, humiliating. This was mentioned at the time and has been ever since. One writer said: "It was bad enough to be conquered and occupied by the mighty empires of the West, the British Empire, the French Empire, but to suffer this fate at the hands of a few hundred thousand Jews was intolerable."

The Western form of anti-Semitism—the cosmic, satanic version of Jew hatred—provided solace to wounded feelings. It came to the Middle East in several stages. The first stage was almost entirely Christian, brought by European missionaries and diplomats. Its impact was principally on the local Christian minorities, where we find occasional recurrences of the previously little-known blood libel. In the fifteenth and sixteenth centuries, this had indeed been explicitly rejected in orders issued by Ottoman sultans. It was now revived on a massive scale. The first major case was the Damascus blood libel in 1840. This kind of anti-Semitism continued to grow, at first on a small scale, during the nineteenth and early twentieth centuries, with a limited response. At the time of the Dreyfus Affair in France, Muslim opinion was divided, some against Dreyfus, some supporting him. A prominent Muslim thinker of the time, the Egyptian Rashīd Riḍā, wrote defending Dreyfus and attacking his persecutors, accusing them not of fanaticism, since they had no real religious beliefs, but of prejudice and envy. Despite this response, one consequence of the affair was the first translation into Arabic of a batch of European anti-Semitic writings.

Then came the Third Reich, with connections to the Arab world and, later, to other Muslim countries. Now that the German archives are open, we know that within weeks of Hitler's coming to power in 1933, the grand mufti of Jerusalem got in touch with the German consul general in Jerusalem, Doctor Heinrich Wolff, and offered his services. It is interesting that the common image of the Germans pursuing the Arabs is the reverse of what happened. The Arabs were pursuing the Germans, and the Germans were very reluctant to get involved. Dr. Wolff recommended, and his government agreed, that as long as there was any hope of making a deal with the British Empire and establishing a kind of Aryan-Nordic axis in the West, it would be pointless to antagonize the British by supporting the Arabs.

But then things gradually changed, particularly after the Munich Conference in 1938. That was the turning point, when the German government finally decided that there was no deal to be made with Britain, no Aryan axis. Then the Germans turned their attention more seriously to the Arabs, responding at last to their approaches, and from then on the relationship developed very swiftly.

In 1940 the French surrender gave the Nazis new opportunities for action in the Arab world. In Vichy-controlled Syria they were able for a while to establish an intelligence and propaganda base in the heart of the Arab East. From Syria they extended their activities to Iraq, where they helped to establish a pro-Nazi regime headed by Rashīd 'Alī al-Gailānī. This was overthrown by the British, and Rashīd 'Alī went to join his friend the grand mufti of Jerusalem in Berlin, where he remained as Hitler's guest until the end of the war. In the last days of Rashīd 'Alī's regime, on the first and second of June 1941, soldiers and civilians launched murderous attacks on the ancient Jewish community in Baghdad. This was followed by a series of such attacks in other Arab cities, both in the Middle East and in North Africa.

While in Berlin, Rashīd 'Alī was apparently disquieted by the language and, more especially, the terminology of anti-Semitism. His concerns were authoritatively removed in an exchange of letters with an official spokesman of the German Nazi Party. In answer to a question from Rashīd 'Alī as to whether anti-Semitism was also directed against Arabs, because they were part of the Semitic family, Professor Walter Gross, director of the Race Policy Office of the Nazi Party, explained with great emphasis, in a letter dated October 17, 1942, that this was not the case and that anti-Semitism was concerned wholly and exclusively with Jews. On the contrary, he observed, the Nazis had always shown sympathy and support for the Arab cause against the Jews. In the course of his letter, he even remarked that the expression "anti-Semitism, which has been used for decades in Europe by the anti-Jewish movement, was incorrect since this movement was directed exclusively against Jewry, and not against other peoples who speak a Semitic language" (cited in Wolfgang Schwanitz, *Germany in the Middle East*, Princeton, 2004, p. 233).

This apparently caused some concern in Nazi circles, and a little later a committee was formed that suggested that the Führer's speeches and his book *Mein Kampf* should be revised to adopt the term "anti-Jewish" instead of "anti-Semitic" so as not to offend "our Arab friends." The Führer did not agree, and this proposal was not accepted. There was still no great problem in German-Arab relations before, during, and even for a while after the war.

The Nazi propaganda impact was immense. We see it in Arabic memoirs of the period, and of course in the foundation of the Ba'ath party. We use the word "party" in speaking of the Ba'ath in the same sense in which one speaks of the Fascist, Nazi, or Communist parties—not a party in the Western sense, an organization for seeking votes and winning elections, but a party as part of the apparatus of government, particularly concerned with indoctrination and repression. And anti-Semitism, European-style, became a very important part of that indoctrination. The basis was there. A certain amount of translated literature was there. It became much more important after the events of 1948, when the humiliated Arabs drew comfort from the doctrine of the Jews as a source of cosmic evil. This continued and grew with subsequent Arab defeats, particularly after the ultimate humiliation of the 1967 war, which Israel won in less than a week.

The growth of European-style anti-Semitism in the Arab world derived in the main from this feeling of humiliation and the need therefore to ascribe to the Jews a role very different from their traditional role in Arab folklore and much closer to that of the anti-Semitic prototypes. By now the familiar themes of European anti-Semitism—the blood libel, the protocols of Zion, the international Jewish conspiracy, and the rest—have become standard fare in much of the Arab world, in the schoolroom, the pulpit, the media, and even on the Internet. It is bitterly ironic that these themes have been adopted by previously immune Muslims precisely at a time when in Europe they have become an embarrassment even to anti-Semites.

What encouraged this development was what one can only describe as the acquiescence of the United Nations and, apparently, of enlightened opinion in the Western world. Let me cite some examples. On November 29, 1947, the General Assembly of the United Nations adopted the famous resolution calling for the division of Palestine into a Jewish state, an Arab state, and an international zone of Jerusalem. The United Nations passed this resolution without making any provision for its enforcement. Just over two weeks later, at a public meeting on December 17, the Arab

League adopted a resolution totally rejecting this UN resolution, declaring that they would use all means at their disposal, including armed intervention, to nullify it—an open challenge to the United Nations that was and remains unanswered. No attempt was made to respond, no attempt to prevent the armed intervention that the Arab League promptly launched.

The United Nations's handling of the 1948 war and the resulting problems shows some curious disparities—for example, on the question of refugees. At the end of the initial struggle in Palestine, part of the country was under the rule of the newly created Jewish state, part under the rule of neighboring Arab governments. A significant number of Arabs remained in the territories under Jewish rule. It was taken then as axiomatic, and has never been challenged since, that no Jews could remain in the areas of Palestine under Arab rule, so that as well as Arab refugees from the Jewish-controlled areas, there were Jewish refugees from the Arab-controlled areas of mandatary Palestine, not just settlers, but old, established groups, notably the ancient Jewish community in East Jerusalem, which was totally evicted and its monuments desecrated or destroyed. The United Nations seemed to have no problem with this; nor did international public opinion. When Jews were driven out, no provision was made for them, no help offered, no protest made. This surely sent a very clear message to the Arab world, a less clear message to the Jews.

Jewish refugees came not only from those parts of Palestine that were under Arab rule, but also from Arab countries, where the Jewish communities either fled or were driven out, in numbers roughly equal to those of the Arab refugees from Israel. Again, the response of the United Nations to the two groups of refugees was very different. For Arab refugees in Palestine, very elaborate arrangements were made and very extensive financing provided. This contrasts not only with the treatment of Jews from Arab countries but with the treatment of all the other refugees at the time. The partition of Palestine in 1948 was a trivial affair compared with the partition of India in the previous year, which resulted in millions of refugees—Hindus who fled or were driven from Pakistan into India, and Muslims who fled or were driven from India into Pakistan. This occurred entirely without any help from the United Nations, and perhaps for that reason the refugees were all resettled. One could go back a little further and talk about the millions of refugees in Central and Eastern Europe—Poles fleeing from the eastern Polish areas annexed to the Soviet Union and Germans fleeing from the East German areas annexed to Poland. Millions of them, of both nationalities, were left entirely to their own people and their own resources.

Some other measures adopted at the time may be worth noting. All the Arab governments involved announced two things. First, they would not recognize Israel. They were entitled to do that. Second, they would not admit Israelis of any religion to their territories, which meant that not only Israeli Jews but also Israeli Muslims and Christians were not allowed into East Jerusalem. Catholic and Protestant Christians were permitted to enter once a year on Christmas Day for a few hours, but otherwise there was no admittance to the holy places in Jerusalem for Jews or Christians. Worse than that, Muslims in Israel were unable to go on the pilgrimage to Mecca and Medina. For Christians, pilgrimage is optional. For Muslims, it is a basic obligation of the faith. A Muslim is required to go on pilgrimage to Mecca and Medina at least once in a lifetime. The Saudi government of the time ruled that Muslims who were Israeli citizens could not go. Some years later, they modified this rule.

At the same time, virtually all the Arab governments announced that they would not give visas to Jews of any nationality. This was not furtive—it was public, proclaimed on the visa forms and in the tourist literature. They made it quite clear that people of the Jewish religion, no matter what their citizenship, would not be given visas or be permitted to enter any independent Arab country. Again, there was not a word of protest from anywhere. One can imagine the outrage if Israel had announced that it would not give visas to Muslims, still more if the United States were to do so. As directed against Jews, this ban was seen as perfectly natural and normal. In some countries it continues to this day, although in practice most Arab countries have given it up.

Neither the United Nations nor the public protested any of this in any way, so it is hardly surprising that Arab governments concluded that they had license for this sort of action and worse. One other example: unlike the other Arab countries, the Jordanians were at that time willing to accept Palestinian refugees as citizens, and the Jordanian nationality law of February 4, 1954, offered Jordanian citizenship to Palestinians, defined as natives and residents of the mandated territory of Palestine—"except Jews." This was clearly stated. There was not a murmur of protest from anyone, anywhere.

These examples may serve to illustrate the atmosphere within which the new Arab anti-Semitism grew and flourished. After the 1967 war, the Israelis came into possession of the former Arab-occupied Palestinian territories, including a number of schools run by UNRWA, the United Nations Relief and Works Agency. These schools were funded by the United Nations. When the Israelis had a chance to look at the Syrian, Jordanian or Egyptian textbooks that these UN-funded schools used, they found many examples of unequivocal anti-Semitism. Although the Israelis could do nothing about anti-Semitism in textbooks in Arab countries, they felt that they could do something about anti-Semitism in textbooks used in schools funded and maintained by the United Nations. The matter was referred to the UN, which referred it to UNESCO, which appointed a commission of three professors of Arabic—one Turkish, one French, and one American. These professors examined the textbooks and wrote a lengthy report saying that some textbooks were acceptable, some were beyond repair and should be abandoned and some should be corrected. The report was presented to UNESCO on April 4, 1969. It was not published.

For those who needed it, all this provided an up-to-date, intellectually and socially acceptable rationale for what ought to be called anti-Semitism but, since that word is not acceptable, might be called Jew-baiting, Jew-hating or generally being unpleasant to Jews.

The rationale has thus served two purposes—one for Jews, the other for their enemies. In anti-Semitism's first stage, when the hostility was based in religion and expressed in religious terms, the Jew always had the option of changing sides. During the medieval and early modern periods, Jews persecuted by Christians could convert. Not only could they escape the persecution; they could join the persecutors if they so wished, and some indeed rose to high rank in the church and in the Inquisition. Racial anti-Semitism removed that option. The present-day ideological anti-Semitism has restored it, and now, as in the Middle Ages, there seem to be some who are willing to avail themselves of this option.

For non-Jews the rationale brought a different kind of relief. For more than half a century, any discussion of Jews and their problems has been overshadowed by the grim memories of the crimes of the Nazis and of the complicity, acquiescence or indifference of so many others. But inevitably, the memory of those days is fading, and now Israel and its problems afford an opportunity to relinquish the unfamiliar and uncomfortable posture of guilt and contrition and to resume the more familiar and more comfortable position of stern reproof from an attitude of moral superiority. It is not surprising that this opportunity is widely welcomed and utilized.

The new anti-Semitism has little or no bearing on the rights and wrongs of the Palestine conflict, but it must surely have some effect on perceptions of the problem and therefore on the behavior and perhaps even on the policies of both participants and outsiders. Nor is the offense all on one side. One might argue that when Arabs are judged by a lower standard than Jews, as for example the minimal attention given to the atrocious crimes committed at Darfur, this is more offensive to Arabs than to Jews. Contempt is indeed more demeaning than hatred. But it is less dangerous.

BERNARD LEWIS is the Cleveland E. Dodge Professor of Near Eastern Studies Emeritus at Princeton University. His most recent books include *Faith and Power: Religion and Politics in the Middle East*, *From Babel to Dragomans: Interpreting the Middle East*, *The Crisis of Islam: Holy War and Unholy Terror*, and *What Went Wrong?: The Clash between Islam and Modernity in the Middle East*, two of which were national best sellers.

Lewis is recognized around the globe as one of the leading authorities on Islam. Hailed as "the world's foremost Islamic scholar" *(Wall Street Journal)*, as "a towering figure among experts on the culture and religion of the Muslim world" *(Baltimore Sun)*, and as "the doyen of Middle Eastern studies" *(New York Times)*, Lewis is a national treasure, a trusted voice whom politicians, journalists, historians, and the general public have all turned to for insight into the Middle East.

HERBERT AND JANE DWIGHT
WORKING GROUP ON
ISLAMISM AND THE
INTERNATIONAL ORDER

The Herbert and Jane Dwight Working Group on Islamism and the International Order seeks to engage in the task of reversing Islamic radicalism through reforming and strengthening the legitimate role of the state across the entire Muslim world. Efforts will draw on the intellectual resources of an array of scholars and practitioners from within the United States and abroad, to foster the pursuit of modernity, human flourishing, and the rule of law and reason in Islamic lands—developments that are critical to the very order of the international system.

The Working Group is chaired by Hoover fellows Fouad Ajami and Charles Hill with an active participation of Director John Raisian. Current core membership includes Russell A. Berman, Abbas Milani, and Shelby Steele, with contributions from Zeyno Baran, Reuel Marc Gerecht, Ziad Haider, John Hughes, Nibras Kazimi, Bernard Lewis, Habib C. Malik, Camille Pecastaing and Joshua Teitelbaum.

INDEX

'Abbasids, in Egypt, 74–76, 98, 116–17
'Abd al-Ḥamīd II, 119
'Abd al-Malik, 78–79
Aden, 126
Afghanistan, xi, xii, 6, 7, 31, 50, 55, 61, 64, 146
  Taliban in, 55
aggression, by Syria/Iran, 24, 29–30
agriculture, in Middle East, 45, 47
Ahmadinejad, Mahmoud, 25, 42, 152
Ajami, Fouad, ix–xiii, xvii–xxvi
Alawis, 34. See also Syria
Algeria, 11, 13, 48–49
'Alī Pasha, Muhammad, 94
Allah, as Islamic God, x, xxi, 11, 25
Al-Nahār (newspaper), 80
anti-Semitism, 155, 158, 161–70
Arab Human Development Report (2009) (United Nations Development Program), 47–48
Arab League, 20, 166, 170–71
Arab states
  aid/donations to, 50–51
  anti-Semitism in, 170
  economies of, 29, 32
  expansionism by, 30–32, 44
  exports of, 48
  investment in, 43, 48, 61
  merger of, 32
  oil/gas resources of, 12, 30, 33, 41–44, 59
  Palestinians and, 23
  population of, 48, 128
  radicalism against, ix–x, xi, xxi, 7–8
  reform of, xxii, 6–7
  regulation in, 48
  subsidies by, 43
  transfer of funds in, 51–52
  U.S. aid to, 50–51
Arab-Israel conflict, 6, 22–23, 26–28, 56–59

Al-Arabiya (television), 116
Arafat, Yasser, 24
Armenia, 3, 50, 81, 92, 96, 118, 126–27, 158
Arnold, Thomas, xxv
Aryan, languages, 140, 161
al-Asad, Bashaar, 29–30, 34
al-Asad, Hafiz, 29–30, 34
Atatürk, Kemal, xi, 10–11, 16
The Atlantic (magazine), xviii
authority
  in Middle East, xi, 124–26
  propaganda against, 124–26
axis of evil, 8
Azzam Pasha, Abdul Rahman, 166

Ba'ath Party, 35, 49, 169
Bahrain, 31
Balkans, xii
Al-Bashīr (newspaper), 96
benign neglect, by U.S., 6
Berlin Wall, ix, 4
bin Laden, Osama, xxi, 7–8
blood libel, 161, 166–67, 170
Bonaparte, Napoleon, 1, 9, 71, 72, 94
Bosnia, 61
broadcasting, development of, 112–13
Busbecq, Ogier Ghiselin de, xix–xx
Bush, George H.W., 2
Bush, George W., xxii–xxiii

caliphate, Islamic, x, 74–75
cartoon, as propaganda, 119
"The Changing East" (Lawrence), 57
Chavez, Hugo, 42
Cheney, Dick, xxii
China, 3, 42, 63–66, 91–92
Christianity
  anti-Semitism, 166
  in Armenia/Georgia, 3
  attacks on, 13
  Crusades by, xix, 13, 21–22, 59